An Atheist Gets the Gita

Rahul Singh is a banker, author and community builder. He is the principal of corporate advisory group at IIM Udaipur and the president of IIM Bangalore alumni association in Singapore. He regularly speaks at corporates and universities at international level on topics that concern millennials such as careers in twenty-first century, conscious capitalism and cross-cultural understanding. He has co-authored *Engineering to Ikigai* and *You Know the Glory, Not the Story*. Brought up in Lucknow, he received a full scholarship to study B.Eng. (Honours) at Nanyang Technological University (NTU), Singapore, and has an MBA from IIM Bangalore.

Galyna Kogut is a researcher with National Institute of Education and has a PhD from NTU, Singapore. She focuses on pedagogy with specific emphasis on language acquisition and teacher professional development. Born in Ukraine, Galyna has widely researched and taught western psychology and eastern philosophies. She has translated various Indian scriptures into Eastern European languages and co-authored *Digital Storytelling for Educative Purposes*. She is the President for Ukrainian club in Singapore and was the founder for Ukrainian Language School, Singapore.

An Atheist Gets the Gita

RAHUL SINGH
AND
GALYNA KOGUT

RUPA

Published by
Rupa Publications India Pvt. Ltd 2021
7/16, Ansari Road, Daryaganj
New Delhi 110002

Sales centres:
Bengaluru Chennai
Hyderabad Jaipur Kathmandu
Kolkata Mumbai Prayagraj

P-ISBN: 978-93-5520-138-6
E-ISBN: 978-93-5520-139-3

Seventh impression 2024

10 9 8 7

Printed in India

Dedicated to Suman Chaki

CONTENTS

Preface: Why Another Book on Gita? *ix*

1. Will This Make Us Happy? 1
2. Fixing an Appointment 4
3. The Lunch 8
4. The Proof 13
5. Dharma 39
6. The Difference between Human and Animal 47
7. What Is the Purpose of Life? 59
8. The Soul 69
9. Time 98
10. The Laws of Karma 112
11. Who Is God? 135
12. Yoga 155
13. What Is Gita? 189

Appendix 199

Notes 224

Bibliography 227

Acknowledgements 229

PREFACE

WHY ANOTHER BOOK ON GITA?

Most books on the Bhagavad Gita are either

- Word-for-word translation from Sanskrit, or
- Lengthy purports and commentaries on each verse, or
- A devotional homage

Currently, there is no book that gives a good overview of the Bhagavad Gita covering key topics in a scientific manner. This book explains the Bhagavad Gita logically in the form of scientific laws and management frameworks. Each chapter has been reviewed by experts in their fields including medical doctors, scientists, lawyers and PhDs in Mathematics, Sanskrit, Engineering and Physics from universities such as Harvard University, Massachusetts Institute of Technology (MIT), Nanyang Technological University (NTU), National University of Singapore (NUS), University of California, Berkley, University of Chicago, Stanford University, Indian Institute of Technology (IIT), Indian Institute of Management (IIM), Banaras Hindu University, Karnataka Samskrit University and Bangalore Medical College.

This book is aimed at people educated in modern western education system who are very unlikely to pick up ancient Indian wisdom. The book serves as an overview of the Bhagavad Gita covering the key concepts of *jiva* (living entity), *Ishvara* (Supreme Controller), *kala* (time), *prakriti* (material nature) and *karma* (causal law) in a very lucid manner. The authors' take on the Bhagavad Gita is that it is nothing but an explanation of how jiva interacts with prakriti in kala governed by the laws of karma designed by Ishvara.

The book is positioned as a dialogue between two IIM graduates, much as the Bhagavad Gita itself is a dialogue, but set in a contemporary modern context. Charan Saket who is 25 years senior to Anveshak Jigyanshu presents rigorous and logical arguments on limitations and expanse of science, definition of proofs, dilemma of ethics and what everlasting happiness means. In the course of the discussion, he covers the essentials of *dharma* (which sustains creation), *atma* (soul), karma and yoga with a crystal clarity on the etymological and epistemological meaning of these terms and their application in the modern world.

WILL THIS MAKE US HAPPY?

Seated in a boardroom on the 27th floor of an office building in Raffles Place Central Business District of Singapore, we deliberated on the theme for IIMPACT—the biggest alumni event in Singapore with over 1,000 attendees. I was the youngest among the eight people in the room having just finished my MBA barely six months back and others in the room had experience of at least a couple of decades. In the middle of the discussion, someone seated at the corner asked, 'But will this make us happier?'

I squinted at him. In my mind I was thinking—either this guy is a deep thinker or mad or probably both. Who comes to a business conference looking for happiness?

The meeting concluded and we dispersed. I found myself taking the same lift as the man who had asked that question. There was an uneasy silence that only lasted for about 10 seconds while the lift came from 27th floor to the first floor (for some reason there is no zero or ground floor in Singapore), but it felt like an eternity. I wanted to strike a conversation and get to know more about this man, but how exactly do you strike a conversation with a complete stranger?

They say when you really desire something, the universe conspires. As the man walked out of the lift pulling the car keys from his pocket, a piece of paper fell out. He didn't notice and moved on. By the time I picked up the paper, he was several feet away from me disappearing into the darkness. I yelled, 'Excuse me, Sir,' bending to grab the paper. He turned and his hazel eyes caught my attention. I quickly ran up to him gasping for breath, 'Sir, seems like you dropped this,' as I tried to get a closer gaze at his face. His receding hairline with a hint of grey suggested he was in his late 40s. Handing the paper over to him and even before he could say thank you, I blurted, 'What do you do?' And as soon as I uttered that, I realized that it was such an awkward and probably rude question to ask a stranger! It showed as if I am only interested in what people do and not in who they are. I cursed myself a thousand times in that brief moment he took to hear my question and respond.

In a calm voice he replied, 'I am a banker'. This answer was not one that I was prepared for and it caught me off guard. Prior to pursuing MBA, I worked as an options broker and as far as I could tell, bankers don't normally ask 'Will this make us happier?' I decided to probe further, 'What do you really do?'

The man was a bit startled. 'Really do?' He asked with a puzzled look on his face.

I realized I owed him an explanation, 'I work for a bank too. What do you really do?'

I felt I made the man uncomfortable and he tried to evade the real question by telling me, 'I am in mergers and acquisitions.'

Or perhaps I was not clear enough and I attempted to explain again, 'Never heard a banker talk of happiness. What do you really do? That question you asked in the meeting is not the one a banker would!'

A moment of silence prevailed, and I understood this

conversation was probably headed nowhere. To weasel myself out of the awkward situation I had self-created, I excused myself by saying, 'Perhaps it is getting late for you. May I have your business card and we can talk at a more convenient time.'

FIXING AN APPOINTMENT

Walking towards the MRT (Singapore's urban rail system), I carefully looked at the business card that was handed over to me a while back. I was deemed too junior to have a business card of my own and my bank had not issued me one. It is amazing how MBA trains you to be a CEO and yet you start as a janitor at the very bottom of the corporate ladder.

I had almost forgotten to tap my MRT card as I bumped into the train station gantry while reading the business card that read, 'Charan Saket, Managing Director, Global Head of M&A'. The train arrived no sooner than I entered the station. It being about 10.00 p.m., which is not a rush hour, I was lucky enough to find a seat and started to google 'Charan Saket'—several links, some news videos and a few images popped up. The third in the list was LinkedIn. I clicked and hit the add button while scrolling down to check his education—IIT Bombay, 1991, and IIM Bangalore, 1995. In my mind, I did some quick calculation, and at rightly guessing his age to be in the late 40s I felt the same joy that perhaps Abhijit Banerjee experienced getting his Nobel Prize.

I looked again at the card and saw a mobile number listed there. I added it to my phonebook and was too tempted to drop a 'Hi'. But then I recalled the three-day rule. When I was an undergraduate at NTU in Singapore, a seasoned senior once told me, 'When you get a girl's number, do not message for the first three days.' Though this wasn't dating, I thought the rule applied nonetheless. Suddenly something struck me, 'Oh no! I didn't even tell Mr Charan Saket my name. So he doesn't even know who I am!'

While I had the luxury of having his business card and deducing his name from it, he didn't even know mine. This thought lingered on for a few minutes and then I forgot about it.

A few days went by and one morning as I woke up in bed, my phone flashed an email titled 'Minutes of Meeting' from the discussion we had earlier in the week on IIMPACT. I immediately remembered the business card. Half asleep, I was thinking, 'Have three days already passed?' Somehow, I convinced myself that since the meeting was on Monday, Wednesday was already the third day.

Walking into the bathroom with phone in one hand and toothbrush in the other, I juggled to WhatsApp, 'Hi! This is Anveshak Jigyanshu. We met in the IIMPACT meeting on Monday' to the number I had saved a few days back. In the next 15 minutes, I finished my morning chores to catch the bus that would bring me to work. I was just in time to avoid being taunted with 'Oh that was early' by my boss.

I spent the morning gazing at Bloomberg screens, replying to a few emails and crunching numbers in an excel sheet. In between, I checked my phone. But there was no reply. I was convinced that I had made a total fool of myself and probably the high flying managing director was happier without me. Suddenly his question, 'Will this make us happier?' seemed to have new meanings and dimensions in my head.

Later in the day, as I walked to grab lunch from Asia Square, I felt a bit dejected at having been ignored. 'How can he ignore me!', 'What does he think of himself', 'Just because he graduated 25 years before me doesn't mean he can be so arrogant,' and a zillion other thoughts raced in my mind. As I was walking back to the office, carrying a Subway sandwich in my hand, I felt my phone vibrate in my pocket. It rains quite often in Singapore and this was one of those afternoons. Both my hands were occupied, one with an umbrella and the other with a sandwich and a drink. Hence I could not pull out my phone. I came back to my office slightly drenched in water and my boss told me, 'Look at that CNH FX swap rollover, I am going to get lunch.' And I knew that meant either eating a soggy sandwich or nothing at all. I pressed Ctrl+Alt+Delete to unlock and look through my screens which resembled a four-winged butterfly with a monitor grip pole in the middle of the four monitors. One FX swap rollover, 21 emails and 53 Bloomberg pings ensured that the lunch went for a toss. I had no time to check what message or call made my phone vibrate.

The rest of the afternoon was pretty uneventful and around 9.21 p.m., I decided that soon it would be too late to be able to get anything from Lau Pa Sat and I better call it a day. Walking towards Lau Pa Sat Hawker Centre, I pulled out the phone from my pocket. I skimmed through a bunch of WhatsApp messages and one caught my attention—Charan Saket. As I was ordering 'Aglio Olio non-spicy' at the hawker centre, I read the message, 'Apologies, I was attending meetings in the morning. Thanks for writing in.' All my negative thoughts about him immediately vanished. I recalled being extremely busy myself in the afternoon and felt bad for all that I had assumed about Mr Charan Saket.

WhatsApp showed 'online' against his name. I quickly

dashed a message, 'I wonder if we could meet for lunch tomorrow—say 12.30 p.m. at China Square?' My Aglio Olio came and I was digging into it while watching a comedy video by a popular Indian stand-up comedian Raju Srivastava. In the middle of the video, I received an 'ok' flashing on top of my screen. He agreed!

After eating dinner, I headed home and had a good night's sleep.

THE LUNCH

Next morning was another battle. We live in strange times where each day, while essentially being no different from the one before, is a struggle—rushing to catch the bus, juggling multiple deadlines at work, working as late as our eyes can tolerate gazing at computer screens and finally crashing on the bed to repeat the cycle.

I was looking forward to the lunch with Mr Charan Saket secretly hoping nothing urgent comes up last minute which would make me cancel the appointment. The clock struck 12.15 p.m. and I decided it was time to escape office and head towards China Square—a 10 minutes walk from my office.

Reaching there five minutes early, I still struggled to find a place for two. Some countries have a lot of space but not enough food while others have abundant food but not enough space. Singapore definitely falls in the latter category. It is nearly impossible to find a seat during peak lunch hours.

As I was looking at the menu at *Fill a Belly* restaurant, I heard a voice, 'Anveshak'. I turned and it was Mr Charan Saket. We exchanged pleasantries and ordered our food. Luckily, just as we finished placing our order, a table near us got vacated. We grabbed it and started talking.

In the course of our discussion, I learnt that Mr Charan Saket had been living in Singapore for five years prior to which he was in various other countries including India, Malaysia and Thailand working with the same organization.

As the food arrived the discussion shifted to happiness.

Mr Charan Saket asked me what happiness meant to me. Without much thinking, in a joking tone, I said, 'Probably a lottery ticket of one million dollars' and laughed about it.

After my laughter subsided, a calm tone asked, 'Why?'

I thought for a while this time and said, 'I can buy a lot of things with it.'

The experienced banker replied, 'More money does not equal more happiness. Even one million dollars will only last as much. It can buy a few things such as a fancy car or perhaps a house, but those things will not be enough to keep you happy for long. It may give you a temporary kick for a while, but very soon you will find yourself in a situation that is no better than it was before winning that lottery ticket. Dr Ann-Christine Duhaime, neurosurgery professor at Harvard University, mentions that as a general rule, our brain tweaks us to want more, more and more. We are constantly running on the hedonistic treadmill and reaching nowhere. There is no end to human desires.[1] When you have one million dollars, you will want a hundred more!'

I pondered and replied, 'What you are saying makes sense. When I was in school I thought getting good grades would make me happy. Those good grades did help me get a full scholarship at a top university but very soon I got used to it. Then when I graduated from NTU, I thought perhaps earning my own money would make me happy. I did get a good job which paid me well but after three years I felt I was lagging and decided to do an MBA. It helped me get an even higher paying job, but I am not sure if I am happier now or if I was happier when I was in the university with almost no money. Now I feel that if I have my own house and a car perhaps I will be happy. There seems to be some truth that the brain tweaks us to want more, more and more. First, I was chasing good grades, then a good job, then an MBA and now a penthouse and a Mercedes. But having said this, who wouldn't love free money—if you win one million dollars out of thin air, it surely will make you happy, wont't it?'

Charan Saket smiled, 'If you ever speak to someone who has won a big lottery or watch interviews of people who have won a big lottery, you will notice how the money they won didn't last and ironically it did not bring them happiness either. One needs to be effort-driven and not result-driven.'

In my head I was thinking what the difference is—doesn't effort lead to results? And what has that to do with happiness or even money?

As if sensing what was going on in my head, Charan Saket said, 'Money which has not been earned through hard work has very little joy attached to it. It gets squandered very quickly. How often have you seen people build billions of dollars of empire only to have their children squabble over it and the wealth disappear in no time?'

Off the top of my head, I could think of at least half a dozen of such billionaire families. Charan Saket continued, 'It is difficult to appreciate the value of something which is not a result of one's own hard work. But as you know hard work alone does not guarantee any result.'

'You are right! In college, I had prepared very hard for an interview with an investment bank which I liked and in the end, I did not get selected. I wondered what was the point of it all? The result did not commensurate with my efforts. I felt so disheartened,' I said.

Charan Saket replied, 'You felt so disheartened because

in your mind you had already fixed the result—getting into the investment bank of your choice. Everything from there went downhill when you did not get your desired result. The word 'desired' is of essence here. When the desired result is not attained, one gets unhappy and when it is superseded, then one feels happy. Anyone who has fixed the result *a priori* has surrendered their happiness to the result. Let's take an example which most of us can relate to. Very often in school, we write exams with the desire of getting atleast a B grade or 80 per cent in it. When the results are declared and we only get C grade or 70 per cent, we feel sad, but if we score an A grade or 90 per cent we feel happy. In this example, we attached our happiness with the result—the outcome of the exam. Fixing the result *a priori* is the root cause of unhappiness. I call this the happiness equation.'

$$\text{Happiness} = \text{Attainment} - \text{Desire}$$

The happiness equation

'Your effort is not the only thing that goes into making the result. There are multiple other factors. Say you prepared very well for an exam, but fell sick on the day of the exam, or in my case I made a very good PowerPoint presentation on a potential acquisition, but I lost the deal because I got stuck in traffic on the actual day.'

I went into deep thinking and after a few seconds of silence, asked, 'Does it mean that our efforts do not matter?'

He responded, 'Of course they do. In fact, our efforts are the only thing that we can control! Let's say you want to have fresh mangoes from your garden. The only way it can ever happen is if you take a mango seed, water it for years, see the plant grow and one fine day you may get mangoes. Your planting the seed and watering is not enough to bear fruits. The seed may never grow or even if it grows, a goat or a cow may eat it up while the plant is still very young or even if it grows to a ripe age, it may catch a disease. You may never see the fruits you desired. On the other hand, if you don't even make the effort of planting the seed and watering it, then it is guaranteed that you will never have mangoes in your garden. Planting the seed is necessary, but not sufficient for you to relish mangoes.'

I was beginning to understand. Charan Saket added, 'When you fix a result, you also open yourself to a variety of vices. The want to achieve the desired result gets so intense that it colours your vision of right and wrong. You can get deviated and go to any length to make sure that the desired result is achieved. Every time we see a student who cheated in an exam or a business executive who falsified data, it is nothing but the desire to achieve results by hook or by crook which is at play. So, my friend, be effort-driven and not result-driven. This is the advice my mentor gave to me when I was your age, along with a book, and this is what I will tell you.'

I nodded in affirmation as I saw Charan Saket look at his watch. I realized that it had been 45 minutes since we had been talking and it was time to head back to work. While walking back I asked him, 'So which book was it?'

THE PROOF

Charan Saket smiled at my question and asked, 'What are you doing this Saturday?'

I responded, 'Nothing.'

'Why don't you come over to my house for breakfast?'

I gladly accepted the invitation as it would save me the hassle of hunting for food over the weekend.

Saturdays are my sleep-as-long-as-you-wish days—essentially make-up for the sleep deprivation throughout the week. A friend of mine who is a sleep expert with a PhD in neuroscience from the NUS had once told me, 'Do not treat your sleep like a bank account. You can't make up for the deficit during the weekdays with credit over the weekends', but I was yet to act upon it. I was turning and tossing in my bed as the sunrays pierced through the window and hit my face. But my body refused to part with the bed. In my head, I was wondering if I was forgetting something, but could not recall what. I felt a little growl in my stomach which jolted my memory, *Oh no! The breakfast was today, right! What time is it now?* This thought sprung me out of the bed and I went straight to the bathroom. It was 8.17 a.m. and I had exactly 43 minutes to not be late for my breakfast invitation.

I ordered a cab before getting into the shower and made it just in time to catch it. A 20-minute ride brought me to one of the most luxurious neighbourhoods of Singapore—Sentosa Cove. My cab stopped in front of a landed house with a swimming pool near the entrance and yachts parked in the bay overlooking the Singapore Strait with Indonesia's Batam Island visible faintly in the background. I must admit that the house looked somewhat intimidating to my 25-year-old self. As I was entering, a thousand thoughts crossed my mind, the most trivial of which was, I hoped my shoes didn't soil the carpet. I somehow felt uneasy as if I didn't belong there.

My uneasiness quickly vanished seeing the jovial smile of Charan Saket as he came to the entrance to receive me. He chaperoned me to the living room and asked me to make myself comfortable on the sofa before excusing himself momentarily. I was scanning the room while he was away. It had a few sculptures on the floor and quite a few obscure-looking paintings on the wall. I had guessed that they were probably quite expensive although I would not pay even ten dollars for them as I lacked the subtlety to appreciate art—could hardly distinguish a Van Gogh from a Da Vinci.

Charan Saket came back with an old-looking book in his hand and taking a seat opposite to me put it on the side table. I was curious to see which book it was, but it was placed with its rear side up so I could not read the name. As Charan Saket asked, 'I hope you did not face any difficulty in getting here,' I shifted my gaze from the book to him. We talked about a few things including me admiring how beautiful his house was before we proceeded for the breakfast. His wife joined us. I learnt that she too was an IIM graduate and a batchmate of Charan Saket. Their only son had finished schooling last year and was studying physics at MIT in the US.

The breakfast was delicious! Crispy dosa dipped in tasty sambhar followed by a generous serving of soft poha and finished off with crunchy jalebi with curd on the side.

After this heavenly food, I could only think of going back to sleep again to make up for my weekly deficit. But I imagined crashing on the sofa was not an option.

After breakfast, Charan walked me to his lawn by the pool. The cool breeze blowing from the seaside wiped off the slumber from my eyes as we sat on a swing. He had that book in his hand and opening somewhere towards the beginning, he showed me a page that had a couple of lines highlighted with a yellow marker. They read: 'You have a right to perform your prescribed duty, but you are not entitled to the fruits of action. Never consider yourself the cause of the results of your activities, nor be attached to inaction.'

Reading this my eyes glittered. I shifted my gaze from the book and looking at Charan said, 'Oh wow! This is so laconic. These two lines contain everything we discussed at the lunch in 45 minutes! Which book is this? It seems to capture a lot in a very few words.' As I was saying this, I turned the edge of the book which he was holding precariously in his hands to reveal the cover. What I saw shocked me—it had a picture of Krishna standing and Arjuna kneeling down!

I was not sure what to say. I was thinking why would someone who is so well educated read a book like this? In a tone that was as questioning as it was confused, I asked, 'Bhagavad Gita?' I added, 'I am a student of science. I don't believe in books like these.'

Charan replied, 'Have you read it?'

I said, 'No. Never felt the need to. What can it possibly tell me that my universities failed to educate me about?' and added, 'This is all fiction and myth, you know? That is why it is called mythology.'

Charan looked at me and smiled, 'You seem to have a

lot of opinions about things you haven't read.'

I felt a little embarrassed, but was not willing to let go, 'What is the proof that it happened?'

'How do you prove something?' he asked.

'By facts and experiments of course,' I said.

'Is it always possible to prove something using an experiment?'

I thought a little and said, 'No, not always. For example, we can't prove that dark matter exists but we postulate it must.'

He explained, 'An experiment is not a proof. It is merely strong evidence in favour of a theory but it is far from proof. Theories such as the theory of evolution, the Big Bang theory or the theory of gravity are just that—theories. You may say that fossils, Hubble Expansion and deflection of light prove these theories, but in reality they just provide strong evidence and not proof per se.'

I continued to listen, flabbergasted.

'We believe that there is a cause for everything. We hold dear that we can deduce the cause by observing the nature around us and we are convinced that the causes, which we call laws of nature, behave in a predictable consistent way. But these are some very fundamental assumptions in science. Moreover, our theories are only as good as our observations. Every time new observations are made, old theory needs revision.

In about 350 BC, the famous Greek philosopher Aristotle believed that gravity acts differently on different objects. He hypothesized that heavier objects fall faster than lighter ones and in direct proportion to their weight. This means a 100 times heavier object would fall 100 times faster. His theory could have been coloured by everyday observation where we see a feather drop slower than say a fruit from a tree. It would take no less than two millennia for cracks to emerge in this theory when, more than 400 years ago, in 1590s, Galileo came up with a revolutionary idea that the time of descent was independent of mass, meaning objects fall at the same speed. He is said to have observed this by dropping objects from the Leaning Tower of Pisa.

Whether Galileo actually did drop objects from the Leaning Tower of Pisa is up for debate, but what we know for sure is that in 1971, Astronaut David Scott of Apollo 15 mission dropped a hammer and a feather on the surface of the Moon and both landed upon the ground in the same time thus disproving, by experiment, what Aristotle hypothesized 2,300 years ago.[2]

Hundred years after Galileo, in 1687, Newton came up with the famous law of universal gravitation published in his book *Philosophiæ Naturalis Principia Mathematica* which further enhanced our understanding of the mysteries of gravity.[3] The formula explains that every particle attracts every other particle in the universe with a force that is directly proportional to the product of their masses and inversely proportional to the square of the distance between their centres.

The first laboratory test on Newton's theory of gravitation would not happen until more than 100 years later in 1798 in the laboratory of Henry Cavendish who is also known for his discovery of hydrogen.[4] We believed the mathematics of Newton's universal law of gravitation was applicable universally. We continued to believe so till we looked at Mercury. And then something changed about the 'universal' application of the universal law of gravitation. The word 'universal' means that the law applies universally. But does it? The universal law of gravitation works pretty well for predicting the motion of objects on Earth as well as for the motion of extraterrestrial planets. It is amazing that the law which explains why an apple falls down on Earth can also predict why the Moon moves around the Earth. In fact, the law works so well that even 300 years later we still use it to send rockets to the outer space.

But for all its wonder, Mercury's path around the Sun does not really follow Newtonian predictions. Mercury is so close to the Sun that it was not until Einstein came up with his theory of general relativity in 1915 that the mystery of the path of Mercury was resolved. Newton's law of universal gravitation lacks temporal quality. It applies instantaneously and this theory held strong for the next 200 years till Einstein predicted that gravity moves at the speed of light.

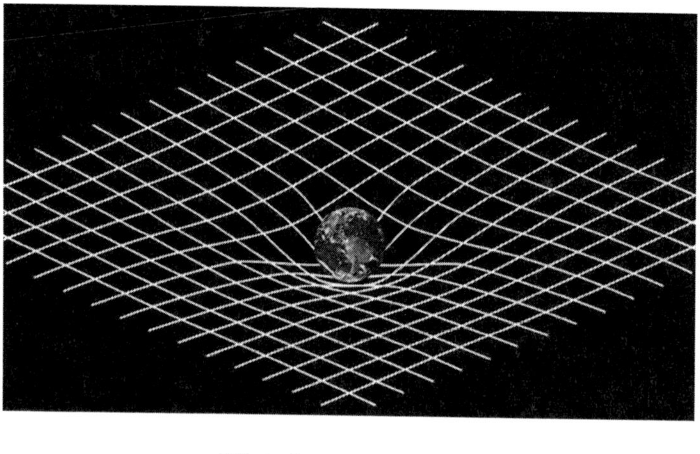

Effect of mass on space-time

Even Einstein's theory fails at singularities such as black holes. The 2017 Nobel Laureate Kip Thorne, the world's leading figure on astrophysical implication of Einstein's general theory of relativity, comments, "The curvature of space-time is so extreme in black holes that Einstein's general relativity fails."[5] Albert Einstein's theory explains a lot, but maybe not black holes. Scientists believe that within the darkness of these massive celestial objects, the laws of the universe fold in on themselves, and the elegant model of gravity laid out in Einstein's general theory of relativity breaks down.

Experimental scientists are pushing Einstein's theory of gravity to its limits by observing far away massive black holes and may start to see cracks in Einstein's theory similar to the one that were exposed in Newton's theory when scientists looked at Mercury. Einstein's theory is an improvement over Newton's but not the complete picture yet. The quest for a better theory consistent with the current observations remains. We haven't tested every star or every planet out there but we believe that the law of gravity applies everywhere. But does it? We also haven't tested the law of gravity at very small subatomic scales due to the limitations of our instruments.

Who knows which Mercury or black hole is out there to expose cracks in every theory we devised so far? We say two hydrogen and one oxygen atoms combine to make water in Russia just the same way as they do in the US. But is that true on Saturn or Venus? Is it true on Alpha Centauri? Have we tested it? Is it true for every place in the universe? Do two hydrogen and one oxygen atom always combine to make water and only water and nothing else? Most likely they will but we don't know for sure what unknown unknowns await us. We have not tested far enough to conclude. As I mentioned to you, observations we make are not proofs, they are merely strong evidence in support of a theory and are far from conclusive irrefutable proof. As and when our observations get finer, every theory comes under the scanner waiting to be tested. Dropping objects from the Leaning Tower of Pisa exposed Aristotle's theory. Mercury exposed Newton's theory. Black holes expose Einstein's theory. We are far from proof, Anveshak.'

Listening to the explanation on the futility of proof, my long-held belief of sacrosanctity of proof got challenged and I asked, 'So what do we mean when we say we have proof?'

Charan said, 'As per *shastras* (scriptures), there are six ways to acquire knowledge or as you like to call it 'prove something'. These are called *pramanas*. In Indian philosophy, pramanas are the means which can lead to knowledge. It encompasses reliable and valid means by which human beings gain accurate and true knowledge. The focus of pramanas is how correct knowledge can be acquired, how one knows, how one doesn't, and to what extent knowledge pertinent about someone or something can be acquired. Pramanas are logical tools that explain why human beings make errors and reach incorrect knowledge, how can one know if one is wrong, and if so, how can one discover whether one's epistemic method was flawed, or one's conclusion was flawed, in order to revise oneself and reach correct knowledge.

The first pramana is *pratyaksha pramana*, meaning one that can be established by direct perception. For example, we can see the Moon with our naked eyes or Saturn's rings using a telescope. An example closer to home would be seeing a river with your own eyes. Pratyaksha pramana is direct knowledge.

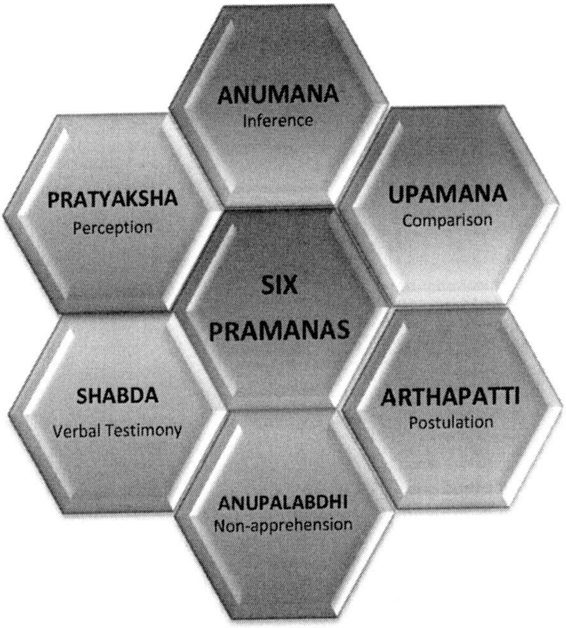

Shad Pramanas or six ways of acquiring knowledge

Next is *anumana pramana* meaning something we can't verify by direct observation but can infer. For example, light coming from far off stars occasionally goes through periodic blips. We don't know for sure but this is attributed to planets orbiting the star. These planets come in between us and the star, causing a decrease in the intensity of light coming from that star. We can't see these planets but we can infer that probably they are there. Another more earthly example can be if you are driving on the road and you hear water burbling, you can infer that probably there is a river nearby although you can't see it directly. Anumana pramana is inferential knowledge.

The third pramana is *shabda pramana* which means something which is believed to be true because of the authority of one who said it i.e., testimony. For instance, when a school geography book states that the Seine River flows through Paris, you can neither see nor hear the river, yet you believe it to be true because of the authority of the book. Shabda pramana is knowledge coming from an authoritative source. The Vedas, Smriti, Puranas and Itihasas are examples of shabda pramana.

The fourth pramana is *upamana pramana* or proof by comparison and analogy. It refers to getting the knowledge of an unknown thing by comparing it with a known thing. For example, most of us have never visited the Moon. So if an astronaut tells us, 'Moon is just like earth but with no air and weaker gravity,' we then have some knowledge of the Moon by comparison or upamana to the earth. If and when we go to the Moon in future, we would be able to relate to the descriptions made by the astronaut.

The fifth pramana is *arthapatti pramana* or postulation, meaning circumstantial implication. The idea is deducing implications from a new fact being cognized, against the background of another fact. In mathematical terms, this is called Bayesian Inference. Suppose we are given two statements as follows: "Statement A: At 12 noon usually the Sun is brilliantly lit in Angola. Statement B: On 21 June 2001, it was pitch dark at 12 noon in Angola." What can we infer from the two statements? The most logical conclusion would be that perhaps there was a solar eclipse at that time. This type of circumstantial implication is arthapatti pramana.

Lastly, *anupalabdhi pramana* is proof by negation or non-perception i.e., the perception of non-existence of a thing. You may be familiar with the word 'upalabdha' which means available. Anupalabdhi means non-availability. It is also known as *abhava pramana*, meaning proof in lieu of the absence of the contrary. The idea is that if something can be observed or inferred or proven as non-existent or impossible, then one knows more than what one did without such information. Anupalabdhi is treated as valid and useful when the other five pramanas fail in one's pursuit of knowledge and truth. An example of this type of proof would be saying, 'No coronavirus antibodies were detected in his blood, so he is free from coronavirus.' As you can see this sort of reasoning, although weak, tells us a bit more of what we know—we have established that as far as detecting via antibodies is concerned, the person does not have coronavirus in his body. But non-detection of antibodies is not a 100 per cent surety of not having coronavirus in the body. Maybe he just contracted the virus a few days back and is yet to develop antibodies. Hence in absence of direct or inferential knowledge, anupalabdhi pramana comes in handy.

Darshana / Pramana	Charvaka	Vaisheshika	Sankhya, Yoga, Vishishtadvaita and Dvaita	Nyaya	Mimamsa	Advaita
Pratyaksha	✓	✓	✓	✓	✓	✓
Anumana		✓	✓	✓	✓	✓
Shabda			✓	✓	✓	✓
Upamana				✓	✓	✓
Arthapatti					✓	✓
Anupalabdhi						✓

Shad Darshanas vs Shad Pramanas

Various schools of Indian philosophy or *darshanas* use these six pramanas to a varying extent in their quest for knowledge. The *Charvaka* school accepts only one valid source of knowledge—direct perception. It holds all remaining methods as outright invalid or prone to error and therefore invalid. The *Vaisheshika* school considers both perception and inference as a valid source of knowledge. *Sankhya, Patanjali Yoga, Vishishtadvaita Vedanta* and *Dvaita Vedanta* schools accept perception, inference and testimony. The *Nyaya* school acknowledges four means of obtaining knowledge i.e., perception, inference, testimony and comparison. *Mimamsa* school considers perception, inference, testimony, comparison and postulation as proper. *Advaita Vedanta* considers all six sources of knowledge of perception, inference, testimony, comparison, postulation and non-perception to be valid.'

'I can understand direct perception method of pratyaksha pramana, inferential method of anumana pramana and also testimonial evidence of shabda pramana. But I am not sure I understand how upamana, arthapatti and anupalabdhi work,' I expressed my cognitive inability.

Charan patiently explained, 'You may have heard of Fermi Paradox. Since time immemorial, humans have wondered "Are we alone?" Looking up at a starry night one often wonders if there are other intelligent life forms in the universe. The 1938 Nobel laureate Italian-American physicist Enrico Fermi pondered the same. There is a contradiction between the lack of evidence for extraterrestrial civilizations and various high estimates for their probability such as estimates from the Drake Equation.[6] There are billions of stars in the Milky Way alone. There is a very high probability that some of these stars have Earth-like planets. Many stars are much older than our Sun and if life is typical on Earth-like planets, then those planets likely have civilizations far more advanced than ours. But why don't we see any evidence of the existence of aliens? We may say, "Since we don't see any evidence of aliens then we must conclude that there are none." This type of reasoning, which relies on the non-availability of evidence, is called anupalabdhi pramana. But this is not the only explanation.

Other theories have also been proposed. One of them is self-destruction theory. Aliens have not contacted us because they ended up self-destroying themselves. The reasoning of this theory is in arthapatti pramana which is inference derived against the backdrop that intelligent life forms like to communicate with other intelligent life forms. If you observe carefully, upamana pramana is hidden in the backdrop statement. We assume "by comparison" that just as homo sapiens like to search for aliens, the aliens like to do the same. Also, we have relied on upamana pramana when we made the inference that they most likely self-destroyed themselves once they reached sufficient scientific progress because we humans do the same—the last century which was industrially the most advanced century so far was also the most violent and self-destructing for mankind.'

I thanked Charan, 'You explained it brilliantly! I never thought of proofs in this way. I can now see your point of six types of proofs. However, I have my reservations against shabda pramana. How can something be taken as proof just because someone said it?' I asked.

'It happens all the time! When your Chemistry teacher tells you that acid mixed with base gives you salt and water, do you not believe it? Or do you rush to the lab to verify first before you believe? When you go to a doctor complaining of malaria and they give you medicine, do you not put faith in the doctor and swallow it? Or do you rush to understand the pharmacology of the drug before taking it? Or do you tell the doctor, "First prove it to me that a mosquito actually bit me, tell me the time when it bit me, tell me how the biting of a mosquito caused malaria inside my body, show me how many paramecia are inside my body? Only then will I take this medicine."

So you see we believe in testimonies all the time without even realizing it. It is not something unique to scriptures. The fundamental premise of shabda pramana is that a human being needs to know numerous facts, and with the limited time and energy available, they can learn only a fraction of those facts and truths directly through pratyaksha pramana and anumana pramana. One must rely on others—parents, family, friends, teachers and ancestors to rapidly acquire and share knowledge. This means gaining proper knowledge either through spoken or written words is shabda pramana. The reliability of the source is important. Legitimate knowledge can only come from the shabda of reliable sources. Shabda pramana is not very different from the modern system of providing references for say university admissions. Universities take the testimony from teachers as a given when deciding to grant admission to a prospective student, don't they?' Charan asked me.

'But don't we need to take shabda pramana with a pinch of salt. What if the teacher's perception of the student is biased?' I questioned.

'All of us are biased. We are all blinded either by our expectations or by our experiences. You must have learnt about these biases in your MBA. Let me show you a chart to refresh what you already know,' he said and pulled up an image chart on his phone.

'This is so much more detailed than what I read during

MBA!' I gasped looking at Charan's phone listing biases such as anchoring bias of over-reliance on the first piece of information we get, bandwagon effect of following the herd mentality, blind-spot bias which is failing to realize one's own flaws, confirmation bias which is only seeing evidence that supports a preset assumption, placebo effect which states that if we believe that something will have a certain effect then we cause it to have that effect, recency bias of overvaluing the latest piece of information, clustering illusion which is a tendency to see patterns in random events.

Charan forwarded me the link to the image on my WhatsApp and said, 'Using these biases we try and come up with a concoction of theories.' He showed me yet another chart and questioned, 'Can you trust such theories which are laden with so much bias?' I looked carefully at the image, which seemed to have listed every framework and model I studied during MBA from goal setting tools to prioritization schemas, to cause and effect frameworks, to problem-solving techniques among others.

'And not only do we have mental biases, even our senses are imperfect. We can hardly see beyond a narrow spectrum or hear beyond certain frequencies. Even what we can see or hear is flawed. As you know our deduction can be only as good as our sense perceptions. Modern science relies on measuring. Even our best instruments are limited by our senses as at the end we interpret that information using our sense organs. The famous theoretical physicist and the 1963 Nobel Prize winner Eugene Paul Wigner noted, "Even if we photograph the stars, we must eventually take in by our senses what the photograph shows. Clearly, all knowledge comes to us ultimately through our senses." Our eyes can only see a very narrow spectrum of wavelengths between 380 to 750 nanometres. It is estimated that we can only see 0.00000000000035 per cent (3.5×10^{-15}) of what is there to see.[7] To put this into perspective, if we take all the seven billion people on earth and collect a million of such earths out of the total number of people in front of us (one million multiplied by seven billion) we would see only 25 people! This is the stunning limitation of the human eye! Similarly, ears can hear only a narrow range of 20 hertz to 20,000-hertz frequency. Even dogs or bats have better hearing than humans. Look at these images. If seeing is believing, then do our eyes cheat us?'

Optical illusions

And then Charan made me listen to a short audio clip on YouTube—https://tinyurl.com/IllusionSound. Fifty-three per cent of over 500,000 respondents reported hearing a man saying the word Laurel, while 47 per cent reported hearing a voice saying the name Yanny. I heard Yanny, while Charan said he heard Laurel. Apparently, it depends on the age of the listener. Younger people are more likely to hear Yanny while older people are more likely to hear Laurel.

Aural Illusion

He elucidated, 'Not only our sense organs have limited range of perception, but they are also prone to illusion. On a sunny day, while driving on the highway we see mirages which look like puddles of water but as we move forward we realize these are just illusions. In school, we performed the experiment of putting a pencil in a beaker full of water and it appeared as if the pencil was broken. The tracks of rail are parallel but appear to be meeting at a faraway point. We tend to hear spooky sounds at quiet nights and are unable to detect taste in food when we have a cold or taste sugar in coffee after eating chocolate. Although wood and metal have the same temperature, when we touch a metal knob of the door on a cold winter night, we feel it is colder than the wooden frame due to the greater heat conductivity of metal. All our five sense organs are prone to errors.

Our material senses have four defects—imperfection, tendency to be deceived by illusions, tendency to commit mistakes and tendency to cheat. I already showed you how our senses are imperfect and susceptible to illusion. We also commit mistakes. With our imperfect senses and our illusion-prone mind, mistakes are inevitable and hence the dictum "To err is human".

For 17 years, from 1998 to 2015, scientists were baffled by microwave radiation at an Australian Observatory in the town of Parkes in News South Wales. They thought it was a message from aliens. Numerous research papers were written on it for years until it was traced back to the microwave oven in the pantry of the observatory![8] You would have heard of the infamous case of Piltdown Man which was a forgery to establish the "missing link" in the theory of evolution. In 1912, scientists claimed to have found the transitional link between ancient apes and modern humans. This excavation by Charles Dawson at Piltdown, East Sussex, England, consisted of human-like skull with the lower jawbone of an orangutan.[9] This was then put in the British Museum and textbooks routinely cited this discovery as evidence of human beings descending from ape-like ancestors. Only in 1953, it came to light that the jawbone was of recent origin and was tampered with to make it look like a fossil. In other words, it was a fraud. The tendency to cheat is sometimes deliberate as in the case with Piltdown Man, but often our senses fool us subconsciously to believe what we want to believe in. We all have cognitive biases.

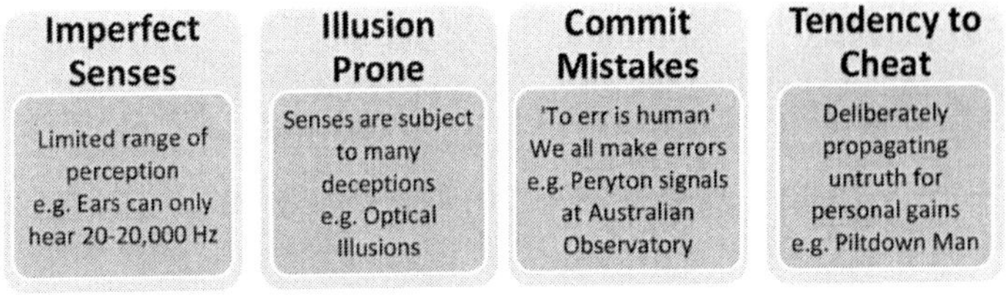

Limitations of our senses

We also like to believe in our own version of the truth. The story of an elephant and blind men tells us that while we may not be wrong, knowledge derived from imperfect and limited senses may not be giving us the full picture. The story is mentioned in Buddhist text Udana 6.4, but it is probably older than that:

> A group of blind men heard that a strange animal, called an elephant, had been brought to the town, but none of them was aware of its shape and form. Out of curiosity, they said, 'We must inspect and know it by touch, of which we are capable'. So, when they found it they groped about it. The first person, whose hand landed on the trunk, said, "This being is like a thick snake." For another one whose hand reached its ear, it seemed like a fan. As for another person, whose hand was upon its leg, the elephant was pillar-like as if a treetrunk. The blind man who placed his hand upon the elephant's side said, "It is a wall." Another who felt

its tail described it as a rope. The last person felt its tusk stating the elephant was something hard, smooth and like a spear.

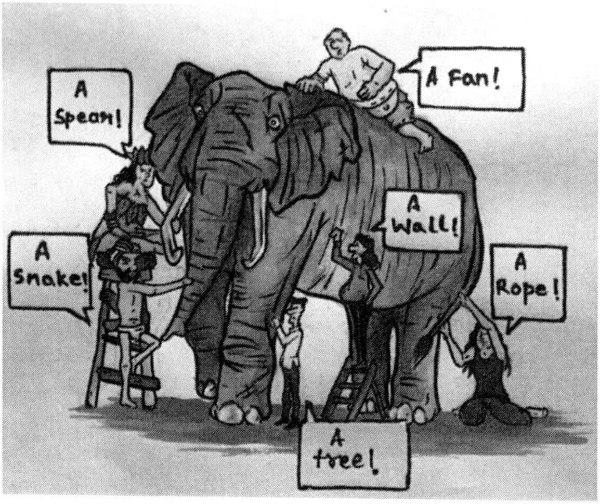

Blind men and the elephant

'As you can see from this story,' Charan continued, 'What we observe may be true only in a limited sense just as each blind man was correct about what the elephant is in a limited sense. The complete truth may be more vast and we may never know it.'

'Never know?' I challenged

'Yes, never! You see even if our senses and our instruments were perfect, we will still not be able to see the vast full truth that is around. Why go further, let's just look at our own universe. It is estimated that the observable universe has two trillion galaxies. Galaxies themselves have around 100 billion stars each on an average. Our own galaxy, the Milky Way, has an estimated 250 billion stars with the Sun being just one of them situated rather on the edge and very insignificant. Light travels at about 3,00,000 km per second and even that takes 1,00,000 years to move from one edge of the Milky Way to the other. As baffling as this is, the observable universe itself is 46 billion light years in radius. It is within this 46 billion light-year radius that we have all these trillions of galaxies, each with billions of stars. Furthermore, the universe is not static but expanding and not just expanding but expanding at a rate faster than light can travel. This means that galaxies are going away from each other faster than light travels.'

'How is that possible? We know that nothing travels faster than the speed of light,' I challenged.

'Well, while that is true, nothing in Physics prohibits the space between galaxies from expanding faster than light can travel. Think of galaxies like dots on a balloon and someone blowing into that balloon such that the dots are getting further away from each other. Interestingly, the rate at which this blowing up is happening is faster than the speed of light! Also, the farther the galaxies are, the faster they are moving away from us. This means that if light starts from a faraway galaxy to reach our Milky Way galaxy, it will never reach us because light is travelling at the speed of nearly 3,00,000 km per second, but the distance between the two galaxies is actually moving apart faster than 3,00,000 km per second! It is like running to the right to catch your friend at the other end of the travelator while the travelator itself is moving to the left. But the travelator is not just moving but moving faster than the speed at which you can run. No matter how hard you try, you can never reach your friend!'

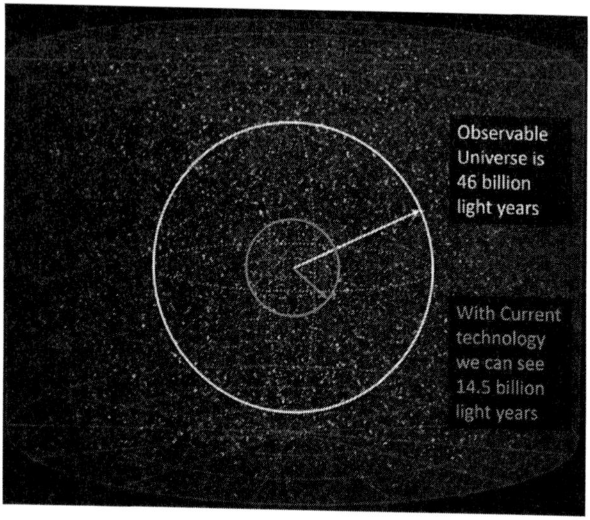

How much can we observe ever?

He continued, 'What the observable universe with a radius of 46 billion light years means is that light which begins from the edge of the observable universe will only reach us 46 billion years later. In the meantime, that galaxy itself will drift away and fall off the edge of the observable universe never to be seen again as it moves away much faster than the speed of light. Every second we are seeing less and less of the universe—we are getting lonelier. Everything is moving away from us!'

'So what is beyond the observable universe?' I asked.

'Probably galaxies identical to the ones we see in the observable universe. But we shall never know because light or any other signal including gravitational waves from there can never reach us. Now, you tell me can we know the big vast truth if we can't even get light or any other information ever to us from what lies beyond 46 billion light years?'

I was awestruck. I was lost for words and tried to shift the discussion in another direction, 'But what about the Bhagavad Gita. Did it really happen?'

Charan replied, 'It is said to have been spoken some 5,000 years ago in 3138 BC.'

'Oh wow! We know these things with such precision?' I was spellbound.

'Yes of course. The precise calculation of time appears in one of the Puranas called Bhagavata Purana which is also known as Shrimad Bhagavatam. If the Bhagavad Gita is about what Krishna said then Shrimad Bhagavatam is about what Krishna did.'

Having listened attentively I probed a bit deeper, 'I have heard stories of Krishna and Arjuna in my childhood in India, but who actually is Krishna and who is Arjuna?'

'Well, the Bhagavad Gita refers to Krishna as Shree Bhagavan which roughly translates to 'the revered Lord' in English. But in reality, there is no word in English which can capture the grandeur of the word 'bhagavan' which essentially is a combination of two Sanskrit words *bhagya* (opulences) and *wan* (possessor) meaning one who has all the opulence. These opulences are described in yet another book Vishnu Purana in verse 6.5.47 as the following six—beauty, wealth, strength, knowledge, fame and renunciation.

aiśvaryasya samagrasya
vīryasya yaśasaḥ śriyāḥ
jñāna-vairāgyayoś caiva
ṣaṇṇam bhāga itiṅgaṇa

—Vishnu Purana (6.5.47)

So Bhagavan is someone who possesses all the six opulences of beauty, wealth, strength, knowledge, fame and renunciation in its entire entirety! People around us who have a little bit more of any of these six opulences than others become immediately attractive to the rest of us. Bollywood actress Aishwarya Rai is attractive because she is more beautiful than most of us. Similarly, Bill Gates is sought after because he has more wealth than a lot of people on the planet. Cricketers such as Sachin Tendulkar or Virat Kohli are admired for their physical strength. Professors and scientists are revered for their knowledge and wisdom. Famous people have charisma due to their prominence. And even Sadhus, hermits and ascetics, who possess nothing, have a huge amount of followers due to their renunciation of the material world. But all these people have just slightly more of what we all have—every one of us has some beauty, reasonable wealth, moderate strength, decent knowledge, modest fame and some renunciation or sacrifice we did in our lives. Yet the moment we see, meet or hear about someone who has any of these qualities slightly above the next-door neighbour, we look up to them in awe and admiration. Now, imagine the glory of someone who has all these six opulences in entirety! This is how Krishna is referred to in the Bhagavad Gita—as Shri Bhagavan. Bhagavad Gita literally means the song of Bhagavan with Bhagavan being Krishna. Arjuna is a prince who has come to the battlefield and is reluctant to fight because he doesn't want to shed the blood of his relatives and teachers who are fighting on the other side. The Bhagavad Gita is nothing but a dialogue between Krishna and Arjuna much as we are having a dialogue right now.'

'It seems like all good things begin with a dialogue,' I joked and added, 'I noticed you said Bhagavan is someone who has all the six opulences. However, your list seems contradictory. How can someone have all the wealth and not be attached to it? Also, from my childhood, I recall that many people in India are referred to as Bhagavan. In my hometown, there lived an ascetic on a small hill. He called himself Tila Bhagavan or literally the Bhagavan on the Hill.'

He responded, 'Anveshak, you see these days it has become fashionable among godmen to use the title 'Bhagavan'. Such people should really think if they have even one of those six opulences of beauty, wealth, strength, knowledge, fame or renunciation in full, leave aside all six! As of 2020, the richest person on earth Amazon Founder Jeff Bezos has an estimated $190 billion to his name.[10] That is 19 followed by ten zeroes. But even this massive concentration of wealth is nothing compared to the overall wealth on earth. Imagine all the gold, silver and diamonds that are there on earth waiting to be mined. And Earth is but a tiny planet in the solar system. Imagine the wealth of the Sun and the valuation of all the energy that the Sun has. Our Sun is just one of at least 100 billion stars in the Milky Way alone. Estimate the wealth of the Milky Way. There are planets in the Milky Way whose entire mantles are made of diamonds. And there are trillions of such galaxies in the universe. Bhagavan owns all of this wealth in these trillions of galaxies comprising billions of stars. He has all the wealth of the universe and yet is not attached to it—that is the elegance of Bhagavan. Renunciation doesn't mean not having! It means having but not getting attached. Detachment is not that you should own nothing, but that nothing should own you! Remember the road to renunciation actually goes through attainment. Only a person who has something can renounce it. One who has nothing has nothing to renounce. We all know the story of Buddha who renounced his kingdom, his wife and his son to seek the truth.'

As I was absorbing the glories of Bhagavan, I asked, 'And what exactly did Krishna tell Arjuna in that dialogue?'

DHARMA

'That dialogue was actually very similar to our dialogue with one important difference,' Charan said.

'And what is that difference?' I asked.

'Unlike our discussion, it was not a leisurely philosophical discussion on a swing with a serene sea in front. It was a discussion right in the middle of a battlefield. Arjuna was not asking questions because he was merely curious. He did not want to pick up some information to be able to talk about it to others and appear very knowledgeable. He wasn't there for an academic purpose. He was asking questions because in the core of his heart he was thirsty; he was hungry for that knowledge because his life depended on it. The greatest war the world has ever known was about to begin. Massive armies had lined up on both sides—seven *akshauhinis* (1,530,900 warriors) on his side and eleven akshauhinis (2,405,700 warriors) on the other side. Each akshauhini comprised 21,870 *rathas* (chariots), 21,870 *gajas* (elephants), 65,610 *turagas* (horses) and 109,350 *pada sainyam* (infantry).

Arjuna was totally bewildered. He asked his charioteer Krishna to take the chariot in-between the two standing armies ready to kill each other. He wanted to gauge the situation from a "neutral ground" with an impartial vision from a no man's land. Arjuna stood in-between the two armies and foresaw the suffering that was bound to take place. He saw thousands of young men dying and their families left devastated. He even recognized friends and well-wishers on both sides. He had his brothers, cousins, elders, grandsire, sons, grandsons, in-laws, relatives and teachers standing in the midst of the armies of both parties. He tried to rationalize and logically explain why he should just leave that place.

He was overflown with compassion, his mind depressed and his eyes full of tears at the destruction that was about to be. Filled with empathy, he declared that the limbs of his body were quivering, his mouth drying up, his body trembling, his hair standing on end and his skin burning. He mentioned that he was unable to stand in the battlefield any longer where he saw only misfortune and was unable to see how any good could come from killing his own kinsmen in the battle. He questioned to what avail was the kingdom, happiness, and even life itself if all those loved ones, for whom one may desire all these, were arrayed on the battlefield of Kurukshetra. He felt that if he relinquished his claim to the kingdom and withdrew from the battlefield, all the problems would be solved and there would be peace without any bloodshed. Ultimately, he was so confused and disorientated that he turned to his charioteer Krishna asking him, "I am confused about my dharma. Please instruct me."'

'So Krishna told Arjuna about dharma? You mean religion?' I asked innocently.

'Not exactly. Dharma is indeed the very first word spoken in the Bhagavad Gita. In fact, Arjuna knew very well what dharma is. It is important to understand what dharma means. It doesn't mean religion! That is a modern mistranslation. The word 'religion' comes from the Latin word '*religio*' which means "to bind". A very crude etymological Sanskrit analogous of that would be yoga and not dharma. Yoga again is very misunderstood to be turning and twisting of the body. Dharma comes from the Sanskrit word '*dharan*' which means something that holds.'

'Holds what?' I interjected.

'Holds anything from falling or disintegrating—so anything that sustains the creation is dharma and what degrades it is *adharma*. There is a story in 'Karna Parva' of Mahabharata, where Arjuna was about to kill Yudhishthira for insulting his divine bow or Gandiva as he had vowed to cut off the head of anyone who disrespects his divine bow. At that time, Krishna gave him the etymological definitions of *satya* (truth) and dharma, to persuade Arjuna that following an oath literally might not guarantee that one was following the path of satya and dharma. He defined dharma as "*dhāraṇāt dharma ityāhuḥ*" meaning that "which holds together, unites and removes separation is called dharma". So, any practice that sustains people/creatures/creation is dharma.

Everything, whether inert (*jada*) or conscious (*chetana*), in the universe has dharma. Dharma at the most fundamental level is *swabhaav* or the innate nature of something. For example, the natural state or dharma of water is to be wet, dharma of fire is to burn and that of sugar is to be sweet. You can take everything away from fire but its ability to burn. Similarly, you can take away everything from sugar but its sweetness and everything away from water but its ability to wet things. If you take away this innate nature or swabhaav then fire won't be fire, water won't be water and sugar won't be sugar. If fire starts to wet, water starts to burn and sugar starts being bitter then that would be adharma. Let's move to the plane of living entities or jivas. Anything that a jiva does which holds the universe's order is dharma and what destroys it is adharma. Jivas have a limited ability to damage this order. How much destruction to the order of the universe can a cow or a tiger or a tree do? Limited, right? But there is one animal which can do great damage. Can you guess which animal that is?'

'Hmm...is it humans?' I guessed.

'Yes, it is humans. As they say, with great powers come great responsibilities. Because humans are more conscious than say a tiger or a tree, they have more power to both sustain and destroy dharma.'

'So what is the dharma of humans?' I wondered

'It is the same! To hold the universe's order,' was the response.

'Same?' I asked bewildered and added, 'Why is it so difficult to follow dharma as a human?'

'To understand this, we need to look *at swadharma, paradharma* and *dharma sukshma*. So *swa* means self and *para* means other. Swadharma and Paradharma are explained beautifully in the Bhagavad Gita (Verse 18.47), which says that it is better to do one's own dharma, even though imperfectly than to do another's dharma, even though perfectly. Meaning if you are a teacher (swadharma), try to do that rather than try to be a doctor (paradharma). You may interpret swadharma as natural temperament. So, essentially, your swadharma is the activity towards which you are naturally inclined.'

'That makes sense. One should follow what one has a natural temperament for. Not following one's heart probably leads to unhappiness. I know so many of my friends from MBA and engineering undergraduate days who are unhappy because they are in jobs that they don't have a natural temperament for. Essentially, they have made paradharma their swadharma,'

I reflected and quizzed, 'And what is dharma sukshma?'

'Dharma sukshma is the reason why the entire Bhagavad Gita had to be spoken. As you yourself mentioned, at the human level dharma starts to get more and more complicated. It is easy to follow dharma in isolation but often various dharmas are at odds with each other. For example, should you tell a lie? No, of course. There is a beautiful story of a sage named Kaushika in 'Karna Parva' section of the Mahabharata. Kaushika never lied. One day, robbers were chasing an innocent man. He hid to save his life. Robbers asked sage Kaushika if he had seen the man. He nodded and showed the robbers where the man was hiding. This resulted in the man's death. Do you think sage Kaushika followed dharma or adharma?'

'I think he did not follow dharma. Although one should not lie. But a truth which harms is not dharma in my opinion,' I replied.

'You are absolutely right! Indeed, Kaushika went to hell despite never lying in his life. The Mahabharata says:

prāṇāntike vivāhe ca vaktavyam anṛtaṁ bhavet |
anṛtena bhavet satyaṁ satyenaivānṛtaṁ bhavet ||
yad bhūta hitam atyantaṁ tat satyam iti dhāraṇā |
viparyaya kṛto'dharmaḥ paśya dharmasya sūkṣmatām ||
satyasya vacanaṁ śreyaḥ satyaṁ jñānaṁ hitaṁ bhavet |
yad būta-hitam atyantaṁ tad vai satyaṁ paraṁ matam ||

—Vyadha Gita, Mahabharata

It means "dharma is truth and adharma is untruth. But when a life is at stake, it is acceptable to tell an untruth. Untruth sometimes leads to the triumph of truth, and the latter declines into untruth. Whichever conduces most to the good of all beings is considered to be truth. Sometimes untruth, which is the opposite of dharma, benefits others—so you see, dharma is extremely subtle. Telling of truth is good, and the knowledge of truth may also be good, but that which conduces to the greatest good of all beings, is known as the highest truth".

Anveshak, this knowledge of subtleties of dharma is called dharma sukshma. Yes, telling a lie is adharma but it is not adharma when a lie is told for the sake of saving a life. Saving a life is bigger dharma. Do you think it is okay to kill?'

'Of course not! Killing is bad. One should never kill.'

'Are you sure about never? Can there be a situation where killing is dharma?'

'Killing can be dharma?' I asked totally confused. 'At least I can't see how killing can be dharma.'

'Very good! You are in fact thinking exactly as Arjuna did. Having learnt from Dronacharya, the greatest teacher of his time, Arjuna knew dharma very well. There were various dharma considerations he had in his mind. His *Kshatriya* (warrior) dharma of upholding righteousness was coming in contrast with his dharma of protecting his family members. His cousins had deprived him of his kingdom and waged a war against him. As a compassionate family member, he did not want to harm them. His compassion was so great that he was not only concerned about his family members but also about the killing of male population in such large numbers in the war (at that time women did not participate in wars). He was concerned that if so many men died in the war then there wouldn't be enough men to take care of families, social constructs would get broken and unwanted progeny might result. He was even willing to rather forego the kingdom that rightfully belonged to him than shed so much blood.'

'As a compassionate human being, he did not want to kill. Wasn't Arjuna right?' I asked.

Charan responded, 'This is exactly where the concept of swadharma and paradharma comes in. The same compassion which is a virtue for a doctor can become an inhibition for a soldier. The duty of the doctor is to save lives and that of the soldier is to kill the enemy. If you send a doctor to fight in the battlefield, his compassion and Hippocratic Oath would inhibit him to kill anyone. There are many doctors who go on battlefields on Red Cross missions. They are not there to kill but to save lives. Similarly, if you send a warrior to an operation table he would not know how to use his sword or knife to save a life.

As a warrior, Arjuna's greatest dharma was to uphold righteousness. Had he escaped from that duty then gross injustice and adharma would reign supreme. Those who sided with the evil including his cousins, grandsire Bhisma and teacher Dronacharya, had to be killed. As we saw earlier, sometimes, lying is dharma. Similarly, sometimes killing is dharma. Essentially Krishna told Arjuna that if he didn't follow his Kshatriya dharma (i.e., to fight against evil) then his cousins would establish gross adharma in the world.

His cousins, the Kauravas, who were a set of hundred brothers (and one sister) had wrongly taken the kingdom which rightfully belonged to Arjuna and his four brothers who were collectively known as the Pandavas. The Pandavas had been tricked in a game of dice in which they lost everything they had, including their wife Draupadi, who was publicly disrobed by one of the Kauravas—Dushasana.

Having lost everything, the Pandavas were ordered to go into exile for 13 years with the last year in *agyatvaas* or incognito. During that last year they were not supposed to be discovered failing which they would have to go away for another 12 years of exile. The eldest Kaurava Prince Duryodhana argued that the Pandavas had been discovered in the last year of their exile and hence had to go into exile for another 12 years. That was not true because as per lunar calendar, the 13 years had concluded five months prior and even according to the solar calendar, six days had passed before the identity of the Pandavas was revealed.

Despite this, the Kauravas, known for their gross adharmic practices, refused to give the kingdom back to the Pandavas. Krishna negotiated on behalf of the Pandavas and argued that the Pandavas were Kshatriya princes whose dharma was to rule. In order to rule, they needed land. He offered that the Pandavas would relinquish their claim to the kingdom and settle for just five villages. But Duryodhana declared that he was not even willing to give the land equivalent to the tip of a needle. Against the backdrop of such gross adharma one may relinquish one's lower dharma of protecting one's family and kill the perpetrator to establish the higher dharma of protecting the subjects of the kingdom from injustice. This dharma sukshma, i.e., the understanding of which dharma is superior, is the summary of what Krishna told Arjuna in that dialogue.'

'Sometimes killing is dharma!' I shall remember this for a long time to come.

THE DIFFERENCE BETWEEN HUMAN AND ANIMAL

I was still absorbing the concept of dharma when Chandrika, Charan's wife, came to the patio and requested us to come inside for lunch. Our conversation had gotten so interesting that I didn't even realize when my breakfast invitation spilled into lunch.

We went in and helped ourselves to generous servings of aloo parathas, paneer and peas curry, basmati rice and daal. Finally, we had ice cream atop gulab jamun.

I started feeling sleepy again after the heavy lunch. This time, I voiced out jokingly, 'The food was so delicious that I think I overate and might need a siesta.'

I was immediately offered by Chandrika to lie down in the guest room upstairs if I wanted to rest. I reluctantly agreed. I dozed off for a while and came back recharged.

Charan asked me if I had a good rest. I replied, 'It is amazing how we spend life eating, sleeping and eating again.'

'Actually, we do two more things,' Charan said smiling.

I asked him what they were.

'Enjoying and defending. And if you think about it, animals are also doing the same four—SEED—sleeping, eating, enjoying and defending. In our everyday life, we do hundreds of activities—getting up in the morning, brushing teeth, bathing, dressing up, going to work, expanding business, eating lunch, building a home, courting others, raising children, enjoying TV, playing sports, listening to music, being busy on social networking, reading books, going for shopping and many more. Yet all this seemingly unending list of activities can be summed up into the four categories or SEED. We eat varieties of food, we yearn for a sound peaceful sleep, we entertain ourselves with books, sports, sex, movies, social media and constantly plan and worry to protect ourselves by building homes, saving for the rainy day, getting insurance and developing weapons. Animals also do the same four activities of SEED.'

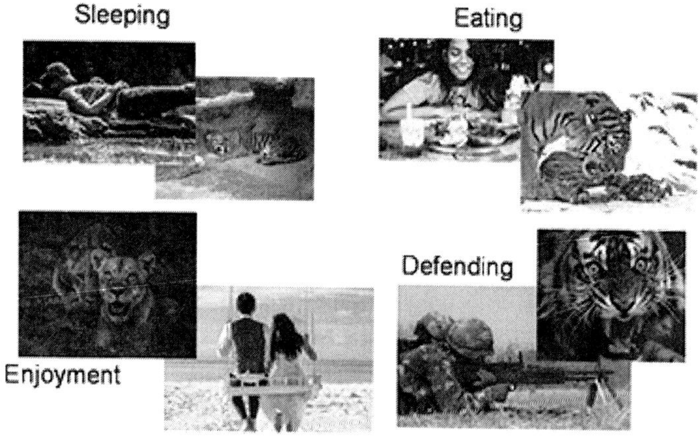

SEED activities

I immediately chipped in, 'Aren't we thinking as well? After all, that is what differentiates us from animals.'

Charan replied, 'Thinking for what? If the only purpose of thinking is to do these four activities of sleeping, eating, enjoying and defending in a better way than animals do then we are no better than two-legged animals. In fact, animals are naturally bestowed to do each of these activities much better than humans—can you sleep as much as a bear, can you eat as much as an elephant, can you mate as many times as a pigeon does in an hour or can you defend yourself as well as a tiger?

Animals can sleep anywhere; we humans on the other hand build stylish beds to lie on. Soft mattresses with latex tops, waterbeds, sleeping pods, hammocks and all sorts of ingenious inventions have been made to make humans sleep better. Even drugs and medicines have been invented to help humans have a sound sleep.

While animals graze and hunt in wild, humans have developed sophisticated ways of indulging in a wide variety of cuisines from Italian pizza to Indian curry, Japanese Sushi, Chinese noodles, Mexican tortillas and Ukrainian borsch. From roadside street food to Michelin star restaurants, we are spoilt for choices to please our palate. The billion-dollar food industry thrives on making the food we eat more presentable and nutritious.

While animals entertain themselves in simpler ways, we have sophisticated means for sense gratification. Even for something as basic as mating, we humans have elaborate rituals and customs. We meet in restaurants, go to movies, engage in shared experiences and finally find emotional and physical enjoyment in each other's company.

Animals rely on their bodies and simple tools to defend themselves. They use claws, teeth, camouflage, poison, pungent odour and other means to protect themselves from becoming preys of a predator. We, on the other hand, use advanced guns, insurance policies, burglar alarms, protective clothing etc., to defend ourselves. Furthermore, we have developed sophisticated and dedicated armies to defend ourselves. The Stockholm International Peace Research Institute estimates that nearly two trillion dollars are spent every year by the nations of the world in military expenditure. Despite all our sophistication, fundamentally we are no different from animals doing the exact same four things—sleeping, eating, enjoying and defending.'

'You mean to say that we are the same as animals doing the exact same four activities you mentioned—sleeping, eating, enjoying and defending?' I asked a bit puzzled and somewhat disappointed at being put at the same level as animals.

'Of course, we are different. As you rightly mentioned we have superior intelligence which allows us to think, reason and question. But what are we using that difference for? The Indian scripture *Hitopadesha* beautifully captures the difference in just one shloka:

āhāra-nidrā-bhaya-maithunāni
sāmānyam etat paśubhir narāṇām |
jñānaṃ narāṇām adhiko viśeṣo
jñānena hīnāḥ paśubhiḥ samānāḥ ||

—Hitopadesha (Verse 25)

It means "both animals and humans share the activities of eating, sleeping, mating, and defending. But the special property of humans is that they are able to engage in spiritual life. Therefore, without spiritual life, humans are on the level of animals." To sum it up, the difference between human and animal is ABCD.'

'ABCD?' I asked with a lost look.

Uniquely Human

A - Ability for Higher Inquiry
B - Bliss Seeking
C - Choice
D - Discriminatory Power

What does it mean to be a human?

'Ability for higher inquiry, bliss seeking, choice and discriminatory power. Human life is precious. It is only in the human form that we have the ability to ask deeper questions beyond SEED—*Athato Brahma Jigyasa.* This first aphorism of Vedanta Sutra means, "Now that you have the human life form, inquire." Have you ever wondered, "Who am I? Why am I here? What is my purpose?"' My eyes lit up and I said, 'Yes I have, sometimes. But the harder I pondered over these questions, the more confused and uneasy I got.'

'These are not easy questions. Unless one studies them in a *parampara,* one may hit a dead end,' Charan replied.

'Parampara?' I wondered.

'Let's say if you want to be a doctor then you go to a medical school, right? You study some theories about human anatomy, pharmacology and physiology. Then under the guidance of a senior doctor, you practice the art of medicine. Similarly, if you want answers to these questions, you must study it under the guidance of someone who has learnt it in a tradition or parampara where a guru has researched on these topics and can give you practical tips for you to have your own realizations.'

I nodded in affirmation.

He continued, 'So while our brain ponders on higher inquiry, our heart yearns for bliss. After all, we all want to be happy. Bliss seeking is a fundamental trait. At the very basic level, we desire sense gratification. This is called *parthiva rasa*. Rasa refers to taste or pleasure, parthiva means earthly or worldly. A dead body is often referred to as *parthiva sharir* which roughly translates to the English term "mortal remains". Hence parthiva rasa refers to bodily pleasures which are experienced through sense gratification of eyes, nose, tongue, ears and skin. This pleasure is maximized when all the five senses are simultaneously aroused. However, this seldom happens in practice. At maximum, we have two or three senses involved.

Food seems tantalizing due to its nice smell and taste. A Michelin star-rated restaurant may add visual stimulation to the food by presenting it in an artistic manner. Similarly, a dance or a movie is pleasing because it engages the ears and eyes with the elegant movements and words of the actors. Aromatherapy massage heightens the sense gratification from touch and smell. Imagine the pleasure which one would experience when all the five senses are engaged with limitless stimulants!

The next rasa is *swargiya rasa* or heavenly pleasure which involves emotional pleasure. Such a pleasure arises from relationships and is a matter of the heart rather than the body. The emotional pleasure we experience on the earth is often alloyed with selfish desires. Unconditional love is hard to be found anywhere in the world. The thing that comes closest to it is mother's love for child.'

I was getting increasingly impatient at the description of bliss and blurted, 'But you said bliss seeking is one of the things which distinguish us from animals. Parthiva rasa and swargiya rasa that you mentioned about seem to be prevalent in animals too. Monkeys roam the jungles in search of sweet-smelling and juicy fruits to experience parthiva rasa. Birds feed their young hatchlings just as humans take care of their newborns offering them swargiya rasa. Aren't they similar to humans in that sense?'

Charan responded, 'Yes they are, but humans can go higher. What really distinguishes humans from animals is not parthiva rasa or swargiya rasa, but the higher taste of *brahman rasa* and *vaikuntha rasa*.'

Hearing those terms for the first time, I gave a puzzled look. Charan understood and explained, 'We love solving problems. All of us were bogged down with some pesky Mathematics problem sometime or the other in school which we could not solve for hours. And suddenly when we got the solution it felt like a eureka moment. As we grow older we get the same pleasure in solving complicated personal or business or intellectual problems.

Animals also solve problems. But they solve simple problems pertaining to the SEED activities. We solve much more complex problems such as how to reach the Moon, how to discover new states of matter or how to find new subatomic particles. None of these are related to SEED.

There is bliss we seek in quenching our curiosity and testing the limits of our intellect. And the biggest question that we are seeking an answer to is why are we here and where do we go? When we solve this problem, we are said to have tasted the brahman rasa or divine knowledge.

Animals do not ponder over such deep questions and hence they never experience the brahman rasa—transcending from the material plane to the spiritual plane. Once we have reached the spiritual plane we are said to have reached vaikuntha or literally a place with no anxiety. Imagine the peace and solace one would feel in a place devoid of all anxieties or worries. Such a bliss is called vaikuntha rasa. As humans we are not content with just parthiva rasa or swargiya rasa which animals also explore. We make deeper inquiries and hence get higher bliss of brahman rasa and vaikuntha rasa.'

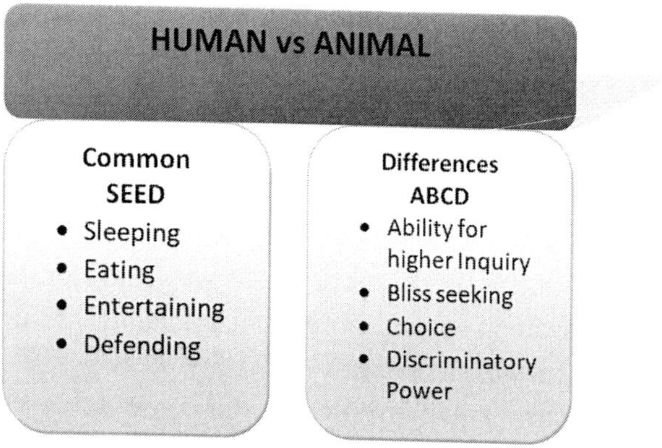

Similarities and differences between human and animal

'And how can we achieve these higher rasas?' I inquired.

'We can achieve them through choices which is the C of our ABCD framework. Animals don't have the luxury of making choices; they simply react to stimuli. We, on the other hand, have advanced intellectual capabilities which enable us to make choices. You may have heard that we have free will?' Charan replied.

'Yes, I have heard that, but I think we don't always have free will,' I responded.

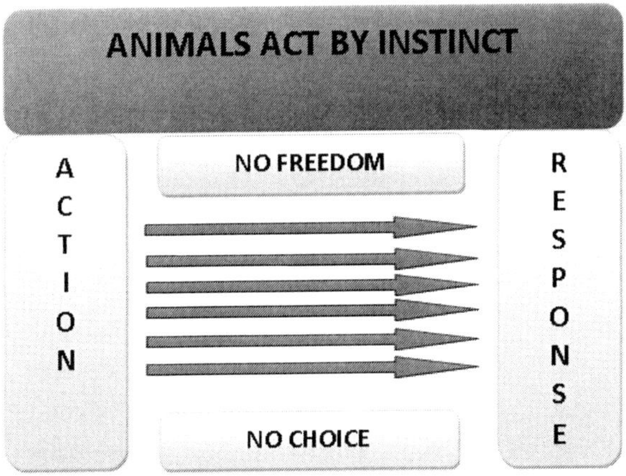

'Actually, you do. We have a rudimentary reptilian brain that operates at the SEED level and an advanced spinal cord which is responsible for us jerking the hand away when pricked with a needle in what is called a 'reflex action'. But beyond this, we have a sophisticated brain that is capable of choosing a response to stimuli.

Unlike animals, we don't simply respond to stimuli on the basis of instinct. If you hit a tiger it will respond immediately. Animals view every other being as prey or predator or mate. They instinctively decide whether to attack a prey or defend against a predator or collaborate with a mate. We also have the same instinct but we are blessed with choice. If you hit another human, they may respond immediately in a form of a punch or may decide to respond later at a place and time of his liking.

We make a choice—to act immediately on instincts or give a delayed response. Animals don't have the higher intellect to ponder over; they act to react to stimuli. You may have read the Holocaust survivor Viktor E. Frankl's book *Man's Search for Meaning* where he says, "Between stimulus and response there is a space. In that space is our power to choose our response.[11] In our response lies our growth and our freedom." There is always a gap between stimuli and response even if it is only a few microseconds—it is in that gap we decide whether to hit back immediately or later. There is always a choice and with each choice we close some path and walk onto another. Life is what we call in mathematics a non-Markovian process—your current state depends on choices you made in the past. The choices may not always be the easy ones nor may we have all the information to make the best possible choice, but there is always a choice.'

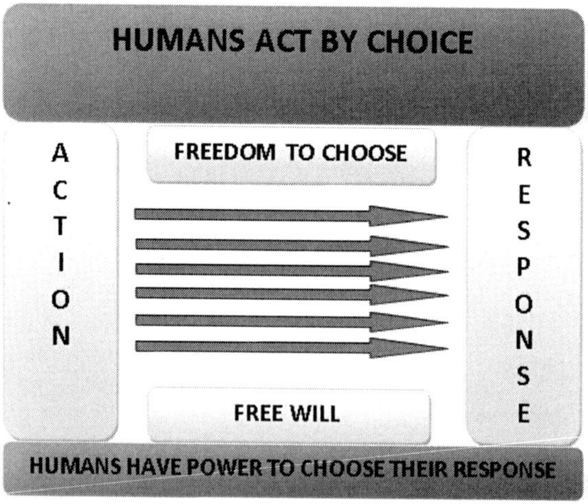

I was totally absorbed in what Charan was saying and reflected, 'But how do we make the right choice? How do we know if it is best to slap now or later?'

He continued, 'Our ability to make the right choices is guided with our power of discrimination—the D of the ABCD framework. In fact, this power of discrimination is the strongest power we have. If you put a banana and a hundred-dollar bill in front of a monkey, the monkey will choose the banana because it does not know that hundred dollars can buy many more bananas. Similarly, when humans are given a choice of money versus health, most end up choosing money over health. They work extra hard, take up high-pressure jobs, stay up all night for days, months and years to earn that extra money only to lose their health in the end. Such humans don't realize that if we preserve health, there will be many opportunities to earn wealth.

Stanford Marshmallow Experiment

There was a famous marshmallow experiment conducted in 1972 by psychologist Walter Mischel, a professor at Stanford University, to study delayed gratification.[12] In the experiment, children aged four to six are offered a choice between one marshmallow immediately or two marshmallows if the child waited for a period of time. The researcher puts one marshmallow on a plate in the room and leaves. The child has a choice—to eat that marshmallow immediately or wait for the researcher to return and give two marshmallows. In the follow-up studies, the researchers found that children who were able to resist the temptation and wait tended to have better life outcomes, as measured by admission test scores, educational attainment, body mass index and other life measures.

It is the power of discrimination that distinguishes a good person from evil, a successful one from an unsuccessful and a wise from a stupid. The Bhagavad Gita talks at length about this when describing the three *gunas* (modes) of *sattva, rajas* and *tamas* (goodness, passion and ignorance). In the very last chapter of the Bhagavad Gita (Verse 18.30), Krishna tells Arjuna about "that understanding by which one knows what ought to be done and what ought not to be done, what is to be feared and what is not to be feared, what is binding and what is liberating". We constantly exercise our free will to make choices. Life is nothing but a series of choices. Our cumulative choices determine where we reach in life. To make proper choices a developed faculty of discrimination is required.'

'But what is the ultimate purpose of all these choices we make? Where are we headed?' I asked.

WHAT IS THE PURPOSE OF LIFE?

'There is only one purpose of all choices we make—no matter how trivial or how profound that choice may be,' Charan replied.

I tried to grasp what he said. Charan explained, 'Let's start with a very simple example. Why are you wearing this T-shirt?'

'Honestly, I put on the first clean T-shirt I laid my hands on this morning.'

'Why is a clean T-shirt important to you?'

'Because it is hygienic.'

'Why is hygiene important to you?'

'So that I stay healthy.'

'Why is staying healthy important to you?'

'Because then I operate better.'

'Why is operating better important to you?'

'Because then I can do things I like.'

'Why is doing things that you like important to you?'

'Because it makes me happy.'

Charan continued, 'You see Anveshak even something as trivial as a T-shirt is linked to our happiness. I could have begun with anything such as why you ate what you ate last night or why you studied whatever you did at the university, yet the final answer of this laddering technique, which you may have learnt in your MBA, would not change. It always ends in "because it makes me happy".'

'So, the purpose of life is happiness?' I asked.

The four purusharthas or object of human pursuits

It seems so! The four *purusharthas* or literally the 'object of human pursuits' comprising *artha, kama,* dharma and *moksha* are all geared towards happiness. Artha refers to economic activities, kama refers to psychological endeavours, dharma deals with moral values and moksha or liberation is spiritual quest. We may however be looking for happiness in the wrong places—chasing temporary happiness instead of eternal bliss.'

'What is the difference?' I asked.

'Temporary happiness is the one we attain by solving temporary problems while permanent happiness is the one we get when we solve real problems,' Charan replied.

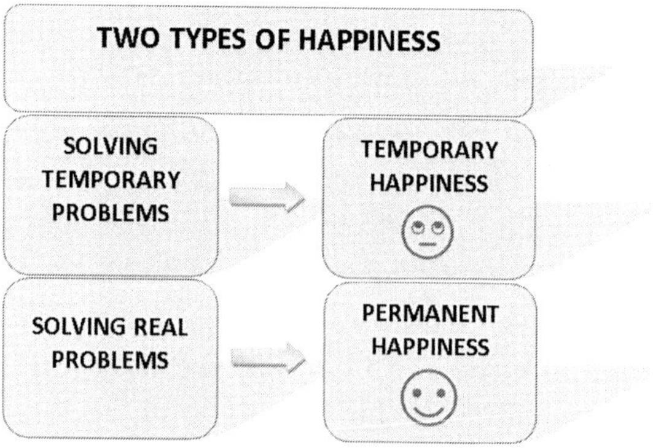

'And what are real problems?' I probed further.

'A real problem has three characteristics: it is common to all, no one wants it, yet no one can escape it. Can you think of any such problem?'

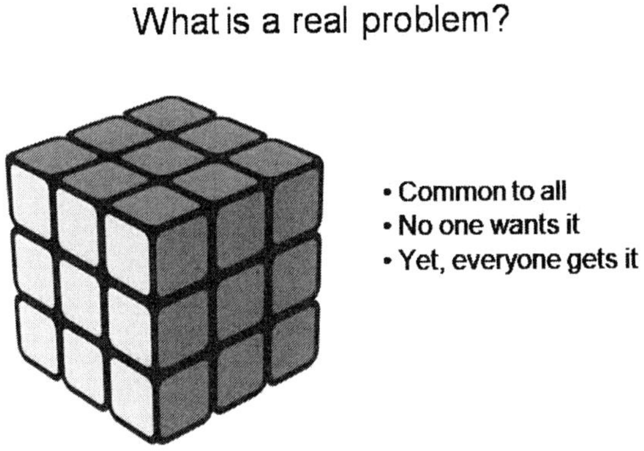
What is a real problem?
• Common to all
• No one wants it
• Yet, everyone gets it

'Death maybe,' I said

'Death certainly is one of them and so is birth. And between birth and death, you have old age and diseases. The Bhagavad Gita (Verse 13.9)—*Janma-mrtyu-jara-vyadhi duhkha-dosanudarsanam*—lists them as the four miseries. These are common to all. No one wants them and yet no one can escape them.'

'Death I understand but why birth? How can birth be a misery?'

'The body goes through six stages of existence in its lifetime—creation as a foetus, birth, growth, maturity, decay and death. If you think being confined in a tiny sack in a braced up position for nine months in absolute darkness being totally dependent on the mercy of another human (mother) is not a misery then we might need to relook at what would qualify as a misery! The Garuda Purana mentions that tied down by the placenta, the foetus does not get much space to move, and its situation is like a bird in a small cage. If death which represents the cessation of life is a misery, then don't you think that by corollary and mirror image principle, birth, which marks the beginning of life, should also be a misery?'

I replied, 'I think the irony of life is that everyone feels they are always miserable no matter what stage of life they are at—when we are young, we have lots of energy and time but no money; as we become adults, we have sufficient money and energy, but no time and when we grow old, we have money and time but no energy. The saying goes that when we come to the world, we are crying and the world around us is smiling; when we leave the world, we are smiling and the world around us is crying. But some people die young. There are babies who die at birth. Is old age really common to all?'

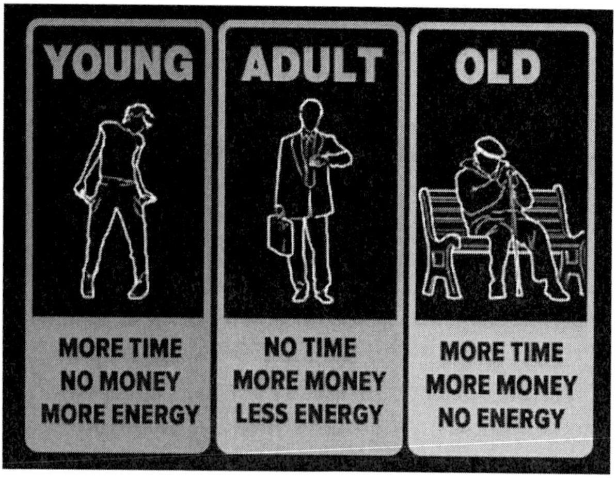

Charan said, 'Let's look at what old age is? Is it chronology or symptoms? Old age is nothing but proximity to death. As one nears death, the body organs start failing. Progeria is a disease that causes premature ageing. About one in every four million babies is born with this defect. They rarely go to live beyond the age of 13 and look very old. Even in so-called sudden death such as accidents, although we cannot see the external symptoms of ageing such as balding head or wrinkles, the internal organs suffer tremendously due to the impact of the accident. If looked at closely, these organs have signs of ageing and ultimately the inevitable happens. Death often comes unannounced and untold. If we look at old age as nothing but proximity to death, then indeed a 90-year-old with 10 more years to live is younger than a child destined to die tomorrow. Similarly, when we see newly born babies die, we might believe that the baby died without suffering any disease or ageing. But upon closer examination, we will see that the baby was not healthy and the organs had symptoms of ageing. No one can escape the four miseries of birth, death, old age and diseases.'

I nodded and asked, 'And what is the source of these miseries?'

'Actually, all problems, whether temporary or permanent, have only three sources—*adhibhautika, adhidaivika* and *adhyatmika*. Problems are either implicated upon us by other living beings or by natural causes or by our own self. There are millions and millions of factors but they can all be classified into one of these three categories. Dengue, malaria, AIDS, flu, war, etc., are examples of adhibhautika i.e., problems caused by other living beings. Shrimad Bhagvatam (Verse 1.13.47) states *jivo jivasya jivanam*, meaning that life forms are dependent on other life forms. Exploitation of a weaker living being by a stronger one is the natural law of existence.

In 2020, the world saw one of the biggest pandemics ever. Globally more than 83 million people suffered of which over 1.8 million died.[13] And all this is due to a tiny coronavirus which measures about 100 nanometers in diameter and weighs just 0.5 femtograms. It takes a billion such viruses to make an average human measuring 170 cm and weighing 60 kg. If you take all the coronaviruses in the bodies of 1.8 million people who have died in 2020 from COVID-19, it will not even weigh one gram! And yet this less than a gram brought humanity to a complete halt in 2020. Millions of people lost their jobs globally, the world's GDP decreased by 4.9 per cent, for the first time in history oil prices went negative, consumer confidence dipped to a historical low and a roll of toilet paper became more expensive than a barrel of oil.[14]

When viruses and bacteria are not troubling us, we have our neighbours or our boss or our colleagues or our relatives or even our own family members who can be a source of our troubles. These are all examples of problems caused by others and hence are adhibhautika.

On the other hand, floods, earthquakes, cyclones, hurricanes, tsunamis and droughts are examples of natural causes or adhidaivika. These are not caused by other beings and are natural calamities. The 2004 tsunami in the Indian Ocean killed an estimated 2,27,898 people in 14 countries including Indonesia, Sri Lanka, India, Maldives, Myanmar, Somalia and Thailand. Similarly, the 1931 Yangtze–Huai river floods in China are estimated to have killed as many as four million people. The cyclone Bhola is estimated to have killed half a million people in Bangladesh and the 2010 Haiti earthquake left 3,16,000 dead.[15]

Besides these, there is yet another source of our problems in this material world. The biggest source of it all—adhyatmika or the problems we implicit upon ourselves. Adhyatmika literally means pertaining to the self. In our mind and body, we keep experiencing ailments, both real and imaginary, which cause bodily suffering and mental anguish. Headache, backache, depression, anxiety, stomach ailments, etc., keep popping up in our bodies from time to time. This world is full of problems and is in fact referred to as *dukhalayam* or abode of sorrows in the Bhagavad Gita (Verse 8.15).

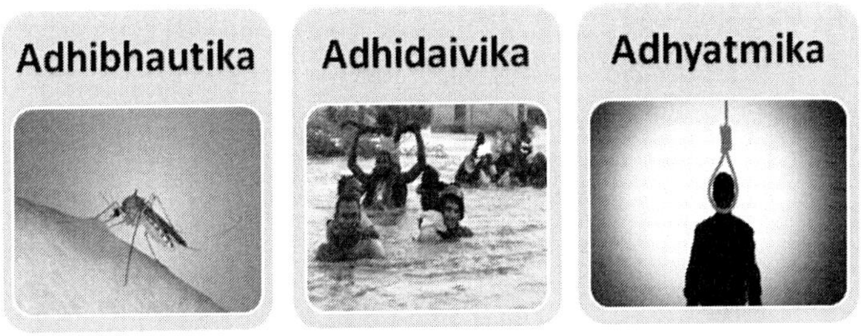

The three sources of miseries

When I was living in Mumbai, a young man in his early 30s died in the house next door. My son was friends with his son and was quite moved by the sudden demise of the father of his friend. To our surprise, my six-year old said that there could be only three reasons for his friend's father's death: either somebody in the house killed him (adhibhautika) or he died naturally from a heart attack (adhidaivika) or he did something to himself (adhyatmika). My neighbour was going through a rough phase in business and recently had a divorce. It turned out that it was a suicide.

For all the might of the human brain and our superior cognitive abilities, it is rather strange that human beings are the only species that die by suicide. Scientifically it has been proven that animals don't willingly harm themselves. History is full of hundreds of examples of famous actors, singers and dancers who entertained the world around them but themselves were so depressed that they died by suicide. The irony of nature is that the most intelligent are also the most tormented.

Our brain is very powerful—within it lies the power to propel us to the celestial heights of space and also to plunge us to the nadir of suicide. Even astronauts who literally go as high as humans can commit suicide. Astronaut (Dr) Chuck Brady, an eagle scout who studied medicine, was a North Carolina football team doctor. He joined the navy, flew into space only to die from self-implicated bodily wounds!'

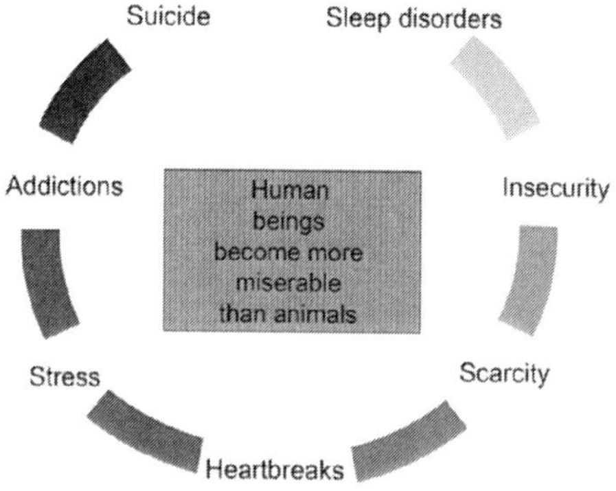

Animals don't experience all this

'The most intelligent among us are indeed the most tormented,' I concurred, 'In my undergraduate days as well as during MBA, I know of friends who committed suicide. One wonders how people who get into such top universities take such a step!'

Charan replied, 'The root cause is unhappiness. For all our material advancements, are we happier? If we look at our modern technological advancements, they have only provided temporary relief and given rise to newer problems. We have followed a painkiller approach to our problems that masks the symptoms temporarily but doesn't remove the root cause.

Temporary solutions have their own use, but should not be treated as permanent solutions. Very often the solutions we invent end up creating bigger problems than the original problem they were meant to solve.

We invented automobiles as a temporary fix for our mobility issues. As per the global status report on road safety by World Health Organization on 17 June 2018, we have 1.35 million people dying in road accidents every year and not to forget many more who die from choking pollution. Not only did we learn how to harness the energy of atoms as a cheap source of energy but we also created the Chornobyl disaster which emitted 400 times more radiation than the Hiroshima bomb and will take at least 300 years to clean.[16] We invented the Internet as an information superhighway to capture the entire humanity's wisdom and now we have issues such as privacy concerns, cyber-bullying, hacking and identity theft. Modern agricultural practices provide fruits and vegetables from all over the globe in supermarkets but this unsustainable farming has also caused massive destruction of forests, soil erosion, and water contamination due to pesticides.

Despite all the advancements in medical sciences today more people are stressed and depressed than ever before. In fact, in medical science this is referred to as the Barsky Paradox—despite the dramatic improvements in healthcare, people are increasingly dissatisfied with their health.

It is ironic how actually undoing everything which used to be the symbol of development in the twentieth century, is defined as development in the twenty-first century—gas-guzzling cars, skylines peppered with factory chimneys, wrapping cities in plastic, are no longer the indicators of development. Today, development means vehicles running on renewable fuel, factories powered by clean technology and biodegradable plastic. Washington-based Worldwatch Institute called the twentieth century the most violent century known in human history with three times more people dead in wars of the twentieth century than in the entire history of warfare between AD 1 and 1899! Shall we call this development?'

I was deeply perplexed and asked, 'What then would be development?'

THE SOUL

'True development is the development of the soul,' Charan replied.

'Soul?' I asked stunned.

'Yes, soul.'

'But what do you mean by soul?' I asked with interest as I didn't believe in soul.

'Have you wondered where we go after we die?' Charan responded.

'That is like asking what happens to computers when they stop running. Well, we go nowhere. We just die and rot,' I explained.

'Are you sure?'

I began to doubt now but I said, 'Hmm...yeah.'

'So when someone dies, why do we say they passed away? Who is it that has passed away? Isn't the body still there?'

'I think that is just wrong usage of language,' I quipped.

'Okay. How about when we say my hand, my leg, my head? Who is this "my" claiming ownership over hand, leg or head? If we are the body which comprises hands, legs and head then why not say "I hand", "I leg" or "I head" where "I" represents the sum total of hand, leg, head, etc.? Is this also the wrong usage of language?'

By now I was utterly confused about the difference between 'I' and 'my'. If one says 'my hand' then it implies belonging. But belonging to whom? If the very hand that I claim is mine is a part of me, then where does "I" end and where does "my" begin?

Seeing me go into a deep thinking mode, Charan came to my rescue, 'See the modern science says we are a bag of chemicals and life is a result of series of transformations of non-living matter. If we are nothing but just a bunch of chemicals then why don't doctors just inject some chemicals into the body of the dead and bring the person back to life? Inert non-living matter suddenly became living when atoms combined to form simple molecules and subsequently complex molecules. The simplest living organism thus born continues to evolve to form more complex organisms. The identification of "self" or "I" is just a combination of atoms and molecules to produce that identity in our heads in the form of consciousness.'

'Yes, and what is wrong with this explanation? That makes perfect sense to me. In fact, didn't Nobel laureate Harold Clayton Urey and his assistant Stanley Lloyd Miller demonstrate that life comes from non-living matter?'[17] I asked.

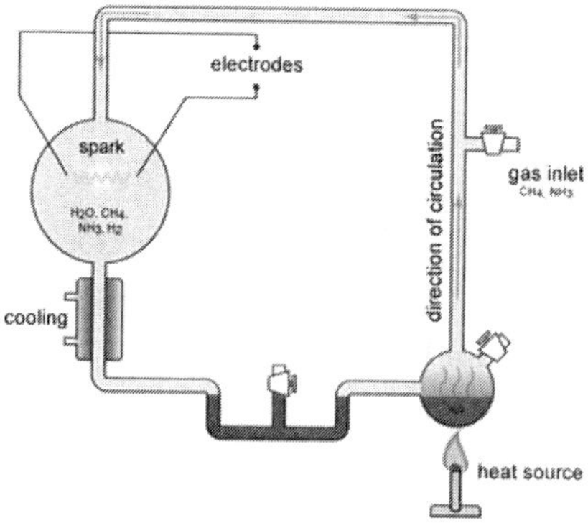

Urey Miller Experiment

Charan replied, 'I am glad you brought up Urey Miller Experiment. Just as the theory of evolution is often misquoted as "humans evolved from monkeys", the Urey Miller Experiment is often misconstrued as "life came from non-living inert matter". Theory of evolution hypothesizes that "monkeys and humans had common ancestors and not that humans came from monkeys". Urey Miller Experiment showed that "simple organic compounds can be formed from gases with the addition of energy" and not that life can be created from inert matter.

The human body is fairly complex with trillions of cells arranged to function brilliantly. Every emotion, every thought, every reality, every imagination and every dream that you ever experienced was perceived by this body. Body is the device through which we experience the world around us, yet we are not the body. The human body is the best chemical factory you know, a mechanical engineer's dream and a computer scientist's ultimate vision. From head to toe, the human body is nothing short of a miracle. Skeleton is a wonderful feat of structural engineering. The circulatory system is the best irrigation system a civil engineer could think of. The kidneys are the best sewage system an environmental engineer could design.

Who created this wonderful machine? Can we recreate it in a lab? Forget the human body, can we even create a single cell? To date, no one has been able to create even the simplest single-celled life using inert matter! People have tried many times and failed all the time. And you want us to believe that from inert matter life was suddenly created—the life that is conscious, life that is aware?

Forget life, it is estimated that the probability of even a simple protein molecule to form randomly from inert matter such as those present in the Urey Miller Experiment is only one in 10^{113}. Any event with a chance of less than one in 10^{50} is considered nearly impossible. The likelihood of it happening even within the period that is hundreds of thousands of times longer than the age of the universe is extremely low. In fact, mathematicians have joked that there is a higher chance of a monkey hitting typewriter keys randomly and generating an entire volume of Shakespeare's plays. And you want us to believe that life did not just get created but continued to evolve to more complex life forms including humans who have 37 trillion cells in them? Does this theory even sound credible to you? There is absolutely no proof that humans evolved from amoeba! We claim God is dead because science has all the answers yet we can't even answer a simple question—where did life come from?'

'Well, there are some missing links. But it is work in progress. Science is trying,' I said in defence.

'Yes, science is trying and there are some good things science has managed to tell us. Such as the body constantly replacing cells—colon cells die after about four days, skin cells live for about two or three weeks, red blood cells live for about four months, white blood cells live on an average of more than a year and almost all the cells in our body are replaced every seven years. The question then is if the body is almost entirely renewed with new cells in seven years then who are we? What is it that makes us us? What is it that is permanent in this ever-changing body?'

I knew where this conversation was heading towards but since I didn't have a counter argument, I continued to listen.

Charan explained further, 'Dr Harry Monsen, Professor of Anatomy at Illinois College of Medicine, has estimated that in a 60-pound person there are about five pounds of calcium, one-and-a-half pounds of phosphate, nine ounces of potassium, six ounces of magnesium and less than an ounce each of iron, copper and iodine.[18] At current prices, it makes the total worth of a human body to be $4. Do you really think we are simply bags of chemicals worth $4?'

'What are we then?' I inquired.

'We are souls,' was the response.

'And what is a soul?' I probed.

'Soul is the source of consciousness. The modern biological view is a materialistic one in which the material body is considered to be the source of consciousness. Consciousness is treated as a byproduct of neuro-chemical reactions inside the brain. In the heterodox school of Indian philosophy, this materialistic view is referred to as the *charvaka* epistemology. On the other hand, the Upanishadic viewpoint is that the soul alone is real and material world perceived is *maya* or illusion,' Charan said.

I immediately protested, 'How can the material world be an illusion?'

Charan explained, 'To understand this, we need to leave the biological interpretation and go to the realm of physics—the world of quantum mechanics. Einstein famously asked, "Do you believe that the Moon exists only when I look at it?" And indeed, if you look at the Copenhagen Interpretation of Quantum Mechanics then it says exactly that reality exists only when it is observed. Without observation, there is no reality, only probabilities, all of which are possible.

Famous French Nobel prize-winning scientist Loius de

Broglie postulated that all matters can be seen as waves.[19] And a wave is nothing but a vibration. Left to themselves, particles would remain as waves until they interact with something else and the wave function collapses to register a unique measurement. Contrary to popular belief, this interaction does not need to be with a conscious observer such as a human. The interaction could be with an apparatus or a human or even with tiny subatomic particles. This interaction is referred to as observation or measurement. So, unless observed, rather than being in one place, matter is located in diffused clouds of waves. So unless observed, rather than being in one precise place, particles behave as waves and are diffused in what can be described mathematically by a probability wave function. This wave function provides the likelihood of finding a particle at a given location.'

I countered, 'But we don't see the world as waves, do we? You exist in front of me in one solid block and not as a diffused cloud of waves.'

Charan said, 'Precisely! But what if my true nature is actually a wave and what you are seeing is but an illusion? After all, my physical body is made up of tiny subatomic particles which are in themselves waves. Hence, my physical body must be a superimposition of those waves. But you can't see me as a vibration because my true wave reality is distorted by illusion or what we call maya in Indian philosophy. When you observe me, you collapse the real quantum wave-like nature of my body to take a distinct shape which you perceive as reality. Even though in truth, I am a wave!

You may have heard about the famous Schrödinger cat experiment. As per the experiment devised by Austrian-Irish physicist Erwin Schrödinger in 1935 in a discussion

Schrödinger cat experiment: Can the cat be alive and dead at the same time?

with Albert Einstein, a hypothetical cat locked inside a box may be considered simultaneously both alive and dead depending on whether a radioactive atom has decayed or not triggering the release of a hammer that shatters a small flask of hydrocyanic acid. The prevailing theory known as the Copenhagen Interpretation of Quantum Mechanics says that a quantum system remains in superposition until it interacts with or is observed by the external world. When this happens, the superposition collapses into one or another of the possible definite states. I exist because you observe. It is by your observation that you are creating an illusion of reality.'

I asked, 'But if you are actually a vibration then why don't I see the true wave-like nature?'

Charan said, 'Because your consciousness is not pure. Soul in itself is *chit* or superconscious. You are an embodied soul with a material body encasing the soul. Hence you are "covered consciousness". If I were to explain to you in terms of physics then I would explain it as follows: we know that matter is a wave until it interacts with another matter. This interaction collapses the wave to take a definite value—this process is called measurement or observation. But what if soul is not material? What if it is not at all made of the same matter as the rest of the universe? Then will the same laws of Physics apply?'

I replied, 'Maybe they won't.'

Charan continued his explanation, 'So that is precisely what it is—soul is spiritual. It doesn't belong to this material world. In fact, soul is an alien in the material universe. For a wave to collapse and be registered as a particle, another matter is needed to interact with it. But since soul is not matter to begin with, no collapsing of wave happens. Hence soul sees the "true nature" of things—which is wave. The material body sees a distorted reality or maya. This distortion or illusion is created when covered consciousness observes the world. This idea of material world being an illusion is expounded in the Niralamba Upanishad of the Yajur Veda:

tapa iti ca brahma satyaṃ jaganmithyetyaparokṣa- jñānāgninā
brahmādyaiśvaryāśāsiddhasaṅkalpa- bījasantāpaṃ tapaḥ

—Niralamba Upanishad (Verse 34)

It says, "True spiritual austerity or tapas is an austerity where the fire of transcendental knowledge, which teaches this material world is an illusion and Brahman is the only reality that burns away the very desire of having opulence possessed by Brahma and other demigods."

Soul is a subtle concept. It is a bit hard to explain in material terms but if I were to give you an analogy then I would say that if we consider our body to be a car then soul is the driver of that car. Of course, nowadays we have driverless cars but traditionally without the driver the car can't move even one inch despite having the same engine, the same horns, the same headlights and the same radiator as in a car with a driver. Similarly, without soul, the body is lifeless despite having the same legs, the same ears, the same mouth, the same eyes and the same brain.

Conceptually you can understand soul as the source of consciousness. It is that which makes the body alive. The extent of consciousness is limited by the type of body which a soul inhabits. It is similar to one person being able to ride at a different speed when using a bicycle versus a car, versus a plane. Likewise, a soul manifests itself differently in different species. When the soul goes inside a bird, it enables the bird to fly, when it goes inside a fish, it propels the fish to swim and when it goes inside a cheetah, it makes the cheetah run just like when electricity goes into a heater it heats, when it goes into the refrigerator, it cools and when it goes into a fan, it moves the blades. Flying, swimming and running are the indicators of soul. If you remove soul, a bird can't fly, a fish can't swim and a cheetah can't run.

Once you remove the soul, the body is as good as a non-living object. When the soul leaves the body, the body will start to deteriorate and rot. This process of removal of the soul from the body is called death. A minute before and a minute after death, the body is essentially the same, but with a difference. Despite having the same lungs, the same brain, the same hands and legs, none of that will function when the soul is removed and the person will be declared dead.'

I chipped in, 'There are many types of deaths. Which death are we talking about—brain death, clinical death or legal death?'

Charan explained, 'Clinical death is the cessation of blood circulation and breathing, the two criteria necessary to sustain life in human beings. Prior to the invention of cardiopulmonary resuscitation (CPR), defibrillation, epinephrine injection, and other treatments in the twentieth century, the absence of blood circulation was historically considered the official definition of death. Today, thousands of people are resuscitated globally each year after being declared clinically dead.

Velma Thomas of West Virginia, USA, holds the record time for recovering from clinical death. She had been clinically dead for 17 hours when she was being taken off life support and funeral arrangements were in progress. However, 10 minutes after being taken off life support, she revived and recovered.[20] With the increasing ability of the medical community to resuscitate people with no respiration or heartbeat, the need for another definition of death occurred, raising questions of legal death.

Today brain death is the legal definition of death. It is the complete stopping of all brain functions. Upon clinical death all tisssues and organs of the body suffer from ischemic injuries caused by diminished or absent blood flow. Most tissues and organs of the body can survive clinical death for considerable periods with bones, tendon and skin surviving for eight to 12 hours. The brain, however, appears to succumb to ischemic injuries faster than any other organ. Brain tissues start dying rapidly after clinical death. Even if the heart is restarted and blood circulation is successfully restored, full recovery of the brain after more than three minutes of clinical death at normal body temperature is rare. Brain injury is the chief limiting factor for recovery from clinical death. Blood circulation in a brain-dead person can only be maintained using life support systems.

Marlise Nicole Muñoz of Texas, USA, was kept on life support machines for nearly two months, despite being brain dead, because she was pregnant and the state of the condition of her foetus was unknown. Brain death is considered to be irreversible. Patients classified as brain-dead can have their organs surgically removed for organ donation. However, in recent times, cases of brain-dead people coming back to life have also been documented.[21] The most famous case is that of 21-year-old Zack Dunlap from Oklahoma, USA.[22] He was declared brain-dead by physicians with his positron emission tomography scan confirming that he was brain dead after a catastrophic brain injury. While his body was being prepared for organ donation, he moved his arm purposely in response to stimuli. Dunlap recovered, went to a rehabilitation hospital, and ultimately went home 48 days later, very much alive. Do note that consciousness i.e., the sense of self-awareness is independent of the body and brain. Even when the brain is not active, consciousness has been recorded.'

'Really?' I asked surprised.

'Yes of course! Thousands of cases have been reported where consciousness has been recorded even when the brain was not active and people were declared dead. As I mentioned to you, the soul is the source of consciousness. So, once you remove the soul from the body, consciousness ceases. At the time of death, the soul leaves together with mind (*manas*), intelligence (*buddhi*) and false ego (*aham*). But if the soul somehow goes back into the body, you will not only regain consciousness but also remember everything that was happening while you were unconscious. It is as if you were observing your own body from outside.

There have been many recorded cases of near-death experience (NDE) or out of the body experience where people experienced consciousness outside of the body.[23] The most comprehensive study of this was done in Dutch hospitals where 344 consecutive cardiac patients who were successfully resuscitated after cardiac arrest in 10 Dutch hospitals were studied. The study compared demographic, medical, pharmacological and psychological data between patients who reported NDE and patients who did not (control group) after resuscitation. In many cases, they noticed that people were conscious even outside of their bodies and reported seeing doctors trying to resuscitate them as they hovered over their own bodies!

In one particular incidence, a 44-year-old cyanotic and comatose patient was brought to the coronary care unit of a Dutch hospital in fully unconscious condition while heart massage and defibrillation were being applied.[24] He needed intubation and it turned out he had dentures in his mouth. The nurse removed the upper dentures and put them onto the 'crash cart'. Meanwhile, they continued extensive CPR. After about an hour-and-a half, the patient had sufficient heart rhythm and blood pressure, but he was still ventilated and intubated, and he was still in coma. He was transferred to the intensive care unit to continue the necessary artificial respiration. Only after more than a week did the nurse see the patient again, once he was moved back to the cardiac ward from ICU. The moment the patient saw the nurse he said, "Oh, that nurse knows where my dentures are" to the shock of the nurse. The patient elucidated, "Yes, you were there when I was brought into the hospital and you took my dentures out of my mouth and put them onto that cart, it had all these bottles on it and there was this sliding drawer underneath and there you put my teeth." The nurse was amazed because the patient remembered this happening while he was in coma and in the process of CPR. When probed further, it appeared that the man had seen himself lying in bed while the nurses and doctors had been busy with CPR.

If the brain is the source of consciousness then how do people have all these experiences while their body is motionless and their brain in an inactive state of coma? Is it possible to see your own body as an observer looking from the outside? How can one remember things when one is in coma or declared dead? There are thousands of such instances across the world which shows that our self-awareness is independent of the body and brain.'

'It is interesting that people can see their own bodies from outside as an observer. But where exactly is the soul located?' I wondered.

Charan replied, 'Point towards yourself.' Before I could grasp what was going on, I saw myself mechanically pointing my index finger towards my heart.

Charan smiled and said, 'The soul is inside your heart.

When I asked you to point towards yourself, then why did you not point towards your beautiful face or your intelligent brain or your agile limbs? Why did you only point towards your heart?'

I sat dumbfounded as Charan continued, 'The soul seated inside your heart is symbolically said to be 1/10,000th the tip of a hair. The Svetasvatara Upanishad (Verse 5.9) mentions *vālāgraśatabhāgasya śatadhā kalpitasya ca bhāgo jīvaḥ sa vijñeyaḥ sa cānantyāya kalpate.* It means "When the upper point of a hair is divided a hundred times and again each such part is further divided into one hundred parts, each such part is the measurement of the dimension of the soul and there are infinitely many such souls."'

I asked further, 'Okay let's say soul does exist, then where does it go after death?'

Charan replied, 'As per the Bhagavad Gita, after death, the soul goes into a new body. The Verse 2.13 says, "As the embodied soul continuously passes, in this body, from boyhood to youth to old age, the soul similarly passes into another body at death." Once the current body is weak and frail, it is of no use to the soul. Just as we change old clothes for the new ones, the soul changes old body for a new one. The process of body becoming weak and frail is called old age and the change of old body for a new one is called death. One who is born is guaranteed to die and one who dies is guaranteed to take birth again.'

I reflected, 'But how do we know that this is actually happening?'

Charan responded, 'Professor Ian Stevenson, the chair of the department of psychiatry at West Virginia in the US, has investigated more than 2,000 cases of reincarnation.

Similarly, India's Dr Satwant Pasricha of National Institute of Mental Health & Neuroscience, Bangalore, has done extensive research on the matter. They both have been documenting some amazing incidences of reincarnation in their respective books.[25] Likewise, American psychiatrist Dr Brian Weiss in his book, *Many Lives, Many Masters*, mentions one of his young patients recalling past life traumas across many lives.[26] Today there are more than a hundred books on reincarnation by highly qualified doctors and scientists.

The Gita makes passing of the soul from one body to next, which is otherwise known as death, a trivial, almost a non-event in the eternal journey of soul. This dramatically shifts the perspective of what life means and how much time we are left with. The soul is eternal. Those who cannot see this eternal nature of the soul are under the constant fear of death—they try to conquer and outlive it. They try to leave a legacy behind—something that reminds the world about them long after they are gone. Death gives a meaning and purpose to their lives by giving them a sense of urgency to create something material while they are still alive. They procreate, build mansions, or set up foundations so that at least something remains after they are gone. Notwithstanding, whatever they create will also not last forever—the children they produce will soon die too, the mansion will crumble and the foundation will run out of funds. Nothing in this world has ever been eternal—not even the body.

As per scriptures, our bodies can be largely divided into three categories—gross body, subtle body and causal body. And the soul is beyond these three.'

Samsara—the cycle of births and deaths

'What does gross, subtle and causal body mean?' I asked.

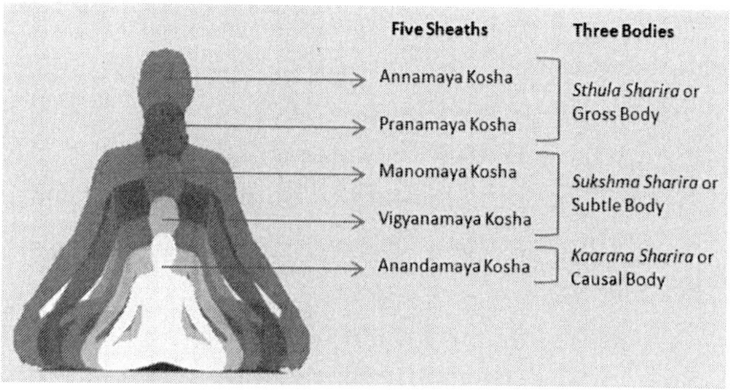

The five sheaths and three bodies

'*Shariratraya* or the doctrine of the three bodies mentions *kaarana sharira, sukshma sharira* and *sthula sharira*. The *Taittiriya Upanishad* discusses five sheaths or *panchakosha* of human body comprising *annamaya kosha, pranamaya kosha, manomaya kosha, vigyanamaya kosha* and *anandamaya kosha* (food sheath, air sheath, mind sheath, intellect sheath and pleasure sheath) in the 'Brahmanandavalli' chapter. Furthermore, the Bhagavad Gita lists 24 elements in the verses 13.6 and 13.7—five *panchamahabhuta* (earth, water, fire, air and ether), *avyaktam* or the unmanifested stage of guna, five object senses (smell, taste, form, touch and sound), five perception senses (eyes, ears, nose, tongue and skin), five action senses (voice, legs, hands, anus and genitals), mind, intelligence and false ego.'

'This sounds interesting. How are the sharira traya, panchakosha and the 24 elements connected?'

'Let's see how these three frameworks of sharira traya, panchakosha and the 24 elements are interlinked. A human being is a biological entity divided into three bodies comprising five sheaths made of the 24 elements. It comes to life when the soul enters.'

'When does the soul enter?' I asked.

'The Garbha Upanishad or literally the Womb Upanishad in the Yajur Veda mentions '*saptame maase jiivena sa.myukto bhavati astame maase sarva sampurno bhavati*', meaning the soul enters the foetus in the seventh month and in the eighth month the foetus becomes complete in every aspect.'

'What happens before the soul enters?' I continued my quest.

'Just like birds make a nest to lay the eggs, human body is being prepared to receive the soul. First the sthula sharira or gross body is formed in the womb. Sthula sharira consists of two sheaths: annamaya kosha and pranamaya kosha. Then comes the sukshma sharira or subtle body consisting of manomaya kosha and vigyanamaya kosha. In addition, there is kaarana sharira or causal body made of anandamaya kosha.'

'What are these different sheaths for?' I inquired further.

Annamaya kosha or the food sheath is called as such because it is nourished by the food we eat. Annamaya kosha includes the five perception sense organs (*sravanadipanchakam*) and the five action sense organs (*vagadipanchakam*) described in the Bhagavad Gita (Verse 13.6). These sense and action organs are made from the panchamahabhuta. Whatever is hard in the body is constituted of earth, whatever is liquid is of water, what is warm is from fire, what moves in the body derives from the essence of air, and the hollow in the body is the essence of space. The earth provides the body with support, the water is necessary for the assimilation of food, the fire essence is for illumination, the wind distributes substances within the body, while ether provides avakasha (or space within). The five perception sense organs of eyes, ears, nose, tongue and skin perceive the five object senses of form, sound, smell, taste and touch. The five action sense organs—hands, legs, voice, anus and genitals—are responsible for five actions of prehension, locomotion, articulation, excretion and procreation. The panchamahabhuta has properties interlinking with the five object senses that are perceived by the five perception sense organs. The Earth has five properties, water has four, fire has three, air has two and ether has just one. Sound, touch, form, odour and taste—these five qualities belong to the earth. Sound, touch, form and taste have been described as the properties of water. Sound, touch and form are the three properties of fire. Air has two properties—sound and touch. Finally, space has only one property—sound.'

I interrupted, 'I can see Earth having all the five properties. I can also comprehend water having four properties. I understand that fire has form or shape, it may have sound sometimes and it can be touched. I also admit that air may produce sound when blowing strongly and may be felt by the skin, but how can space have the property of sound? We know that a medium is needed for sound to travel. Sound does not travel in space.'

Gravitational waves

Charan replied, 'Yes indeed, I had learnt the same thing in my high-school science—sound doesn't travel through space.

And I vehemently believed in it. It seems like the scriptures are lying, isn't it? Well, in 2016, we discovered gravitational waves—two black holes of 29 and 36 solar masses merging about 1.3 billion light years away. Gravitational waves are waves of stretching and shrinking space. In essence, gravitational waves vibrate the spacing between masses. These waves look like a sound and they sound like a sound because they are sound! These waves were amplified a billion times and were indeed audible to human ears as chirps. It might be time to revise the high-school science textbooks.'

I replied, 'I was aware of these gravitational waves but did not know that they were audible. It is amazing how science keeps getting updated every decade or so.'

Charan responded, 'Science keeps getting updated but scriptures don't. Whatever was said or written thousands of years ago remains static in time. Whether we are able to verify it or not, using our current understanding of science, is a different matter altogether.'

'It is amazing how Garbha Upanishad mentions about the development of foetus. We only learnt about this recently in science using sophisticated tools such as ultrasound. I now understand annamaya kosha and its relations with the panchamahabhuta, what are the other four koshas for?' I asked.

'Beyond the annamaya kosha, the scriptures talk about the pranamaya kosha i.e., vital energy or air sheath, which comprises five components called *pranapanchakam*—*prana* (respiration), *apana* (evacuation of waste from the body), *vyana* (blood circulation), *samana* (digestion) and *udana* which is reversal functions such as ejection of unwanted substances from the body including actions such as sneezing, coughing, vomiting, etc., in emergency situations. At the time of death, it is udana, which essentially is reversal of life processes, that ejects life from the body.

If you think of the body as a computer then the annamaya and pranamaya kosha together are like the hardware of the computer or sthula sharira. They can be touched and felt. As we know, the computer also has software. Beyond the sthula sharira is the sukshma sharira or subtle body—the seat for *antahkarana* or inner instrument. This is like the software of the computer. The antahkarana comprises manomaya kosha and vigyanamaya kosha. The manomaya kosha consists of manas or mind (responsible for response to stimuli from sense organs, memory and self-doubt) and the subconscious. The vigyanamaya kosha is responsible for intelligence. Also seated in the antahkarana is false ego or *ahamkaara*. Just like software cannot be touched or felt, similarly, the manomaya and vigyanamaya koshas comprising mind, intelligence, subconscious and false ego can't be touched or felt. They can only be perceived, and hence they are called subtle body or sukshma sharira.

But why does this computer (i.e., the subtle and the gross bodies) comprising the hardware (annamaya and pranamaya koshas) and the software (manomaya and vigyanamaya koshas) exist in the first place? What is the need for this computer? The answer lies in the kaarana sharira or the causal body which is the cause or the seed of the subtle and gross body. The cause is the desire of the soul to enjoy the material world. Once the soul has this desire, anandamaya kosha or the sheath of enjoyment comes into being. Ananda means enjoyment. It is just like the desire of a scientist to create a calculating machine that gives rise to a computer consisting of hardware and software. The kaarana sharira becomes the genesis of the subtle body comprising manomaya and vigyanamaya koshas and the gross body comprising pranamaya and annamaya koshas. It is the desire of the soul to enjoy the material world that is the cause or the kaarana of the other two shariras—shukshma and sthula.'

'I noticed the ending "maya" in all the five koshas you mentioned—what is maya?' I quizzed.

'Maya, you may have heard, can roughly be translated to illusion. As you rightly pointed out all the five koshas are called maya. This is because they are layers of illusion that prevent us from identifying our true self—the atma. All these layers of maya arise from *avidya* or ignorance—the ignorance of not identifying ourselves with the soul but assuming that we are the body. By the process of elimination—referred to as *neti neti* in Sanskrit meaning "not this, not that"—we can see that we are not the annamaya kosha which is the gross body nourished by food, we are not the pranamaya kosha where various vital processes take place, we are not the manomaya kosha where instincts reside, we are not the vigyanamaya kosha where intelligence dwells and we are not even the anandamaya kosha which is the sheath of enjoyment. So what are we if we are none of the above? We are the atma beyond all these five koshas of material world which are illusions.'

I nodded and probed further, 'Thanks for such a structured explanation of body and soul. I also noticed that you are referring to manomaya and vigyanamaya as separate entities—are they not one and the same thing? When we say someone is intelligent or we say someone has a sharp mind, isn't it the same?'

'The Sanskrit word for mind is manas and that for intelligence is buddhi. People often confuse the two but these are two very different faculties. Let me explain it to you with an example. So let's say you are diabetic and you love sweets. If you are given sweets, your mind or manas will tell you to eat them while it is your intelligence or buddhi which tells you, "Don't eat—you are diabetic." The body discriminates and knows by buddhi. The body responds to stimuli, remembers, fancies and thinks through manas. Scriptures define buddhi or intelligence as the ability to discriminate between choices by taking decisions based on free will with the determination to pursue the choices we make. Without intelligence, we are just highly sophisticated information processing machines.'

I interjected, 'But don't we now have artificial intelligence (AI) capable of making intelligent decisions?'

Charan continued, 'The word 'intelligence' in AI is a misnomer. AI has no discriminatory power to make choices based on free will. It simply does what it is programmed to do—see patterns in large chunks of data referred to as Big Data, elicit insights from the data and make informed decisions based on patterns it learns. For sure, AI learns and can make logical decisions. In fact, it can make better decisions than humans as it is not coloured by biases that humans are so prone to. But it does so without any free will or determination. It is a slave which executes the program it is programmed for—observe data, find insights, make decisions. It lacks a buddhi. Without a buddhi, it doesn't have a will of its own.

The Katha Upanishad explains the distinction between manas and buddhi brilliantly. It mentions about Vajashravasa, a renowned sage, desiring a boon from the demigods. The sage performed *yajna* wherein he vowed to sacrifice all his possessions in *sarva dakshina* which means donating everything one has. However, his son Nachiketa noticed that his father was less than forthcoming in his donations. Vajashravasa was only donating the cows that were old, barren, blind or lame. Nachiketa approached his father and reasoned that he too was a possession of his father and asked to which god his father intended to donate him. Peeved by this question, in a fit of rage Vajashravasa said, "I will give you unto Dharmaraja Himself!" Dharmaraja, also known as Yamaraja, is the lord of death. He is called Dharmaraja because upon death he evaluates whether the person followed dharma or adharma. He examines the pious and vicious activities done by a person and punishes or rewards accordingly.

Hearing his father's wish to offer him to the lord of death, the obedient son Nachiketa headed straight to Dharmaraja's home, but the god was out. He waited for three days without any food or water. In Indian culture, a guest is akin to god—*atithi devo bhava.* Upon coming back, Dharmaraja felt very sorry that his guest had to wait in hunger and thirst. Pitying the child he gave him three boons.

For the first boon, Nachiketa asked for peace for his father and himself. Next, he asked Dharmaraja to teach him how to perform the sacred fire sacrifice. And finally, for the third boon, he asked Dharmaraja to tell him what comes after death of the body. Dharmaraja was quite reluctant as the mystery of what comes after death had never even been revealed to the demigods. He persuaded Nachiketa to ask for some other boon and offered him many material gifts. However,

Nachiketa rejected all of them citing that any material gift Yamaraja would give would be ephemeral and would not last forever.

Left with no option and because he had already made a promise, Dharmaraja elaborated on the nature of the true self (atma or true ego), which persists beyond death of the body. In Katha Upanishad (verses 1.3.3–1.3.17), Dharmaraja explains Ratha Kalpana or chariot analogy of the senses, mind, intelligence and soul to Nachiketa. Dharmaraja elaborates on the hierarchy of various levels of existence using the allegoric expression of an individual as a chariot. The body is equated to a chariot where the horses are the five senses or *indriyani*, the reins are the mind, and the charioteer is the intellect. The master of the chariot is the self or atma or true ego.

Ratha Kalpana

If the intellect, which is the driver of the chariot, lacks the power of discrimination then the mind becomes uncontrollable and is pulled in all directions by the senses which are like the vicious wild horses. When the mind is overpowered by any one of these senses running wild, one loses the ability to reason, and becomes like a ship tossed by storms upon high ocean. Upon forgetting the true nature of who the master of the chariot is (soul), the intellect or buddhi becomes entangled in the field of action or karma and falls into *samsara* or the never-ending cycle of births and deaths.

The same concept is illustrated again in the Bhagavad Gita (Verse 2.67): "As a boat on the water is swept away by a strong wind, even one of the senses on which the mind focuses can carry away a man's intelligence." In the Bhagavad Gita (Verse 6.34), Arjuna reflects, "The mind is very restless, turbulent, strong and obstinate. It appears to me that it is more difficult to control the mind than to control the wind." Furthermore, Krishna tells Arjuna in the Bhagavad Gita (Verse 6.6), "For him, who has conquered the mind, the mind is the best of friends; but for one who has failed to do so, his mind will remain the greatest enemy." So unless the driver of the chariot, the intellect, knows how to control the mind reins, the senses will pull the mind towards all kinds of temptations.'

'Thanks for beautifully explaining the difference between mind and intelligence. I remember you mentioned ego earlier. What is ego?' I asked.

'When the soul enters the body it does so along with mind and intelligence, and thus a false ego is born. False ego is the juncture of spirit and matter. As the spiritual soul enters the material body, an illusion develops which makes the soul believe that it is just this body and nothing apart from the body. This illusion is indeed very strong. Do you know of anyone who is not attached to this body? Is there a person who doesn't fear death? Have you ever met anyone who is not struggling to keep the soul and body together? It is not easy to let go of this mortal body. Even those who die by suicide fear death. They get so afflicted by their current situation and view their future with such hopelessness that they come to see death as an act of escaping their pain and suffering. This fear of death also gives us what is called survival instinct. We learn how to take care of our body and defend it against adversities. We eat, sleep and even mate only to defend this body. Mating ensures that even when we stop existing, a part of us survives as our children. The soul's attachment to the body is very profound. This false identification of the self with the body and not the soul is called false ego or ahamkaara.

The combination of the eternal spiritual soul with the perishable material body is indeed the genesis of this false ego. What is even worse is that this sense of ego doesn't just stop at the body. 'I' (aham) becomes 'me' (ahamkaara) and me becomes 'mine' (*abhimaana*). Ahamkaara is the ego that makes us believe that we are the doer instead of *nimittamatra* or the mere instrument in everything that is happening to us and around us. We start feeling that we have the supreme control over what lies in store for us, whereas the bitter truth is that we are merely one of the many factors in whatever results come from our efforts. We can control our efforts but not the results. However, our sense of false ego makes us believe that we are the supreme doer.

Ahamkaara soon gives way to abhimaana. The body adorns clothes and starts having a sense of belonging with the cloth—my cloth. This sense of belonging or abhimaana keeps growing. We find partners and say "my wife or my husband". We have children with our partners and call the offspring "my children". We acquire some wealth and say "my money". We get some job and say "my job". We become CEOs, presidents or prime ministers and start saying "my company or my country". We start thinking of ourselves as the possessor and forget that we are nimittamatra. This possessiveness has been compared to licking honey off the sword's edge—it tastes sweet just for a moment and then it is painful all the way.

Our sense of self keeps ever-expanding—from my body to my clothes, to my wife or husband, to my money, to my work—and the beginning of all this is associating one's identity with the body as opposed to the soul. We become very territorial about this ever-growing identity of self-protecting our body, our loved ones, our belongings. We are ready to fight over it. We fight to keep the body alive. We fight over property and we fight over who should be the rightful owner. When someone encroaches on what we feel is ours, we feel violated. Our sense of ahamkaara compels us to fight back. As long as we keep seeking external validation to establish our self-identity, we are entrapped in the false ego identifying ourselves with body, with gender, with titles, with designations, with caste, with nationality or with our relationship with others, be it our boss or co-worker, brother or sister, father or mother, son or daughter, giver or taker, teacher or student, etc.

None of these is our true identity. False ego means false identity or temporary identity. It is the view that "I am this body—thin, fat, short, tall, male, female, black, white and so on." Or that "I am rich, poor, Indian, American, religious, atheist, student, teacher and so on." The thin can get fat, the fat can get thin, the short can grow tall, the tall can lose some height as they grow old, the male can surgically become female, the female can get operated to become male, the black can become white, the white can become tanned, the rich can get poor, the poor can get rich, the Indian can take up American citizenship, the American can take up Indian one, the student can become teacher, the teacher can become student, the atheist can become religious and the religious can become atheist. Thoughts, opinions and feelings change all the time. Amidst so many changes, who is the real you? Is there an unchanging reality behind all these identities of body, nationality, profession, wealth or religious preference which is not subject to the vagaries of time? Only when we look internally and realize the true meaning of self as soul have we really found our true ego or true meaning of aham.'

'So you mean our real identity is the soul and not the body?' I asked puzzled.

'Absolutely!'

TIME

No sooner than Charan uttered 'absolutely', his wife called us in for tea. What began as a breakfast for me had now extended all the way to 3.00 p.m. high tea. I sheepishly told him, 'I don't know how time just passed away so quickly.'

He joked, 'Well, as Einstein says: "When you sit with a nice girl for two hours you think it's only a minute. But when you sit on a hot stove for a minute you think it's two hours. That's relativity." I am well aware I am not a nice girl.' We both had a good laugh while sipping Indian masala tea with revitalizing cardamom aroma and strong ginger flavour as he continued, 'Time is what prevents everything from happening at once.'

'Wow! That is a brilliant one,' I exclaimed

'It has to be. After all, it is said by the same Einstein. And since you mentioned time, there is a famous quote on time by J. Robert Oppenheimer who cites the Bhagavad Gita.'

'You mean Oppenheimer, the inventor of atomic bomb?' I wondered.

'Yes, the very same Oppenheimer. Not only had he read the Bhagavad Gita but he also understood about the subtleties of kala which in Sanskrit means both time and death: "I remembered the line from the Hindu scripture, the Bhagavad Gita. Vishnu is trying to persuade the Prince that he should do his duty and to impress him takes on his multi-armed form and says, 'Now I am become Death, the destroyer of worlds.' This was a quote from the Bhagavad Gita:

śrī-bhagavān uvāca
kālo 'smi loka-kṣaya-kṛt pravṛddho
lokān samāhartum iha pravṛttaḥ

—Bhagavad Gita (Verse 11.32)

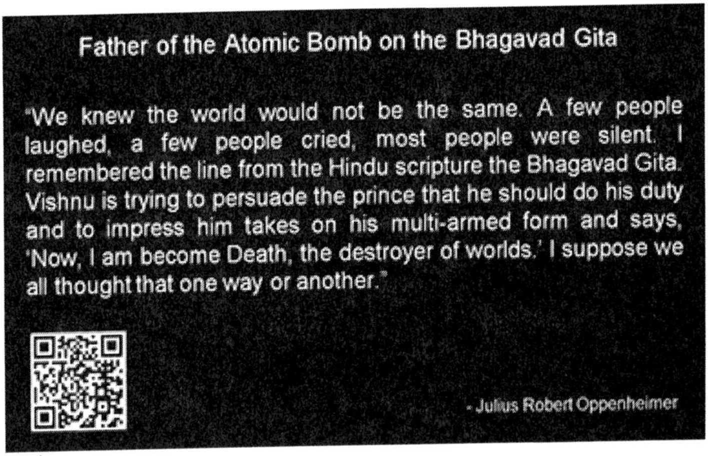
Father of the Atomic Bomb on the Bhagavad Gita
"We knew the world would not be the same. A few people laughed, a few people cried, most people were silent. I remembered the line from the Hindu scripture the Bhagavad Gita. Vishnu is trying to persuade the prince that he should do his duty and to impress him takes on his multi-armed form and says, 'Now, I am become Death, the destroyer of worlds.' I suppose we all thought that one way or another."
- Julius Robert Oppenheimer

Oppenheimer on the Bhagavad Gita

In fact, time is nothing but the twenty-fifth element of the universe. You might recall the 24 elements I mentioned to you earlier as per the Bhagavad Gita (verses 13.6 and 13.7)—five panchamahabhuta, *avyaktam* or the unmanifested stage of guna, five object senses, five perception senses, five action senses, mind, intelligence and false ego. The scriptures mention that these 24 elements come into being only when and because the twenty-fifth element of time is infused into the universe by the creator. The creator is considered to be beyond time. In fact, the creator is considered both the beginning and the end of time. While everything in the material universe is affected and impacted by time, the creator is out of the realm of time. If you think of this universe as a matrix or a video game then the creator is not the character in the game but the player and also the creator of the game! The creator exists in a different sphere unimpacted by time because the creator is the very genesis of time itself.'

'Kala or kaal, meaning both time and death, seems appropriate to me. After all, what separates birth from death if not time? Eventually we will all die,' I reflected.

'Yes and no,' Charan replied.

'What do you mean?' I asked.

'Our material bodies will die but soul never dies. Beyond the 25 elements of the universe is the eternal soul which is not material and is spiritual in nature. The Bhagavad Gita (Verse 2.20) states, "The soul is neither born, nor does it ever die; nor having once existed, does it ever cease to be. The soul is without birth, eternal, immortal and ageless. It is not destroyed when the body is destroyed." And Verse 2.23 explains further, "The soul can never be cut to pieces by any weapon, nor burned by fire, nor moistened by water, nor withered by the wind."'

'Interesting. I was under the impression that everything in this universe and even the universe itself comes to an end. At least that is the idea of Big Crunch—the universe began with Big Bang and will collapse with Big Crunch,' I tried to reason.

'This is correct, but only for the material world. Soul is actually an alien in this material universe—it is spiritual in nature. In fact, the Big Bang and Big Crunch you are talking about is mentioned in the holy scripture, Shrimad Bhagavatam or Bhagavata Purana. It says, our universe will last 311 trillion years and we are currently right in the middle of this time period. And even when the universe is finished, the soul will still be around as it is not material.'

'Wow! 311 trillion years. That is too precise! How did you come up with that number?'

'Oh for that I will need to tell you how time is measured as per our scriptures. The smallest unit of time mentioned in the scriptures is *truti,* which is much smaller than a second, and the largest is one life of Brahma, which is much larger than 13.7 billion years, the age of the universe. Chapter 11 of the third canto of Shrimad Bhagavatam mentions:

aṇur dvau paramāṇū syāt trasareṇus trayaḥ smṛtaḥ
trasareṇu-trikaṁ bhuṅkte yaḥ kālaḥ sa truṭiḥ smṛtaḥ
śata-bhāgas tu vedhaḥ syāt tais tribhis tu lavaḥ smṛtaḥ

—Shrimad Bhagavatam (Verses 3.11.5–3.11.6)

It means "two atoms make one double atom, and three double atoms make one hexatom (*trasarenu*). The time duration needed for the integration of three trasarenus or motes is called a truti, and 100 trutis make one *vedha*. Three vedhas make one *lava*".

Furthermore, it goes on to describe longer and longer units of time, "The duration of time of three lavas is equal to one *nimesa,* the combination of three nimesas makes one *ksana,* five ksanas combined together make one *kastha,* and

15 kasthas make one *laghu*. Fifteen laghus make one *nadika*, which is also called a *daṇḍa*. Two daṇḍas make one *muhurta*, and six or seven daṇḍas make one-fourth of a day or night, according to human calculation. It is calculated that there are four *paharas* (intervals) in the day and four in the night of a human. Similarly, 15 days and nights are a fortnight, and there are two fortnights, white and black, in a month. The aggregate of two fortnights is one month. Two of such months comprise one season, and six months comprise one complete movement of the Sun from south to north. Two solar movements make one day and night of the demigods, and that combination of day and night is one complete calendar year for the human being. The human being has life duration of 100 years."'

I was aghast at such precise description of time and I wondered, 'But how did they measure such small units of time? Did they have atomic clocks?'

'For the longest time, one second was defined as 1/86,400th part of a day. This definition came from the fact that a day was historically divided into 24 hours with each hour comprising 60 minutes made up of 60 seconds each. Since 1967, one second has been defined as exactly "the duration of 9,192,631,770 periods of the radiation corresponding to the transition between the two hyperfine levels of the ground state of the caesium-133 atom (at a temperature of 0 K)". Although very precise, this definition is so abstract that hardly anyone can make any intuitive sense of it.

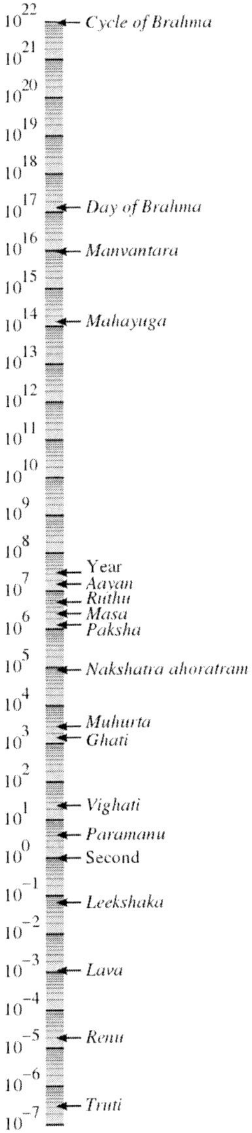

Units of time

Shrimad Bhagvatam descibes a practical unit of time that could be measured directly in any household—nadika (equals 24 minutes). It describes the usage of a kind of an hourglass to measure nadika; the measuring pot for one nadika or daṇḍa can be prepared with a six-pala (14 ounce) pot of copper, in which a hole is bored with a gold probe weighing four *masa* and measuring four fingers long. When the pot is placed on water, the time before the water overflows in the pot is called one daṇḍa. As you can see this measurement is much more intuitive to understand as compared to the definition of one second based on Caesium-133 atom.'

I nodded my head in acknowledgement and circled back, 'And 311 trillion years? How did we get that?'

'Large units of time are measured in terms of *yugas*. Each yuga which is also known as *mahayuga* comprises four smaller yugas—*Satyayuga*, *Tretayuga*, *Dwaparayuga* and *Kaliyuga* in the ratio of 4:3:2:1 with Kaliyuga being the smallest and Satyayuga being the largest. Altogether, a mahayuga is 10 times (4+3+2+1) the duration of Kaliyuga. Kaliyuga lasts 1,200 divine or *deva* years. A day for devas or demigods is equal to one year of humans. This implies that one divine year is equal to 360 human years. This makes one Kaliyuga duration equal to 4,32,000 (360*1,200) human years and one mahayuga, which is 10 times the duration of Kaliyuga, equal to 4,320,000 years.

One day of Brahma, the creator of the material universe, has 1,000 such mahayugas or is as long as 4.32 billion years. His night is equally long. During Brahma's night, the universe is annihilated and during the day it is restored. At the end of Brahma's life, the universe gets totally destroyed. If you do a bit of math, you will conclude that with 1,000 mahayugas in a day of Brahma plus the same duration at night and him living for 100 years, each year comprising 360 days, the life of the universe is 311 trillion years (2*1000*4.32 million*360 days*100 years). We are in the middle of this 311 trillion year-long life cycle of Brahma. Or in other words 155.5 trillion years have passed since the creation of our universe.'

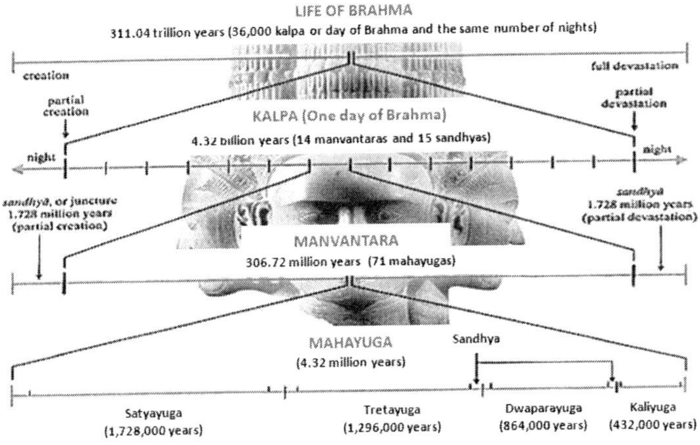

Yuga Cycles

I was lost in the numbers Charan just quoted but then I recalled something from my Physics classes, 'But wait a minute! This doesn't make any sense. After all, we know from science that the universe is 13.7 billion years old and not 155.5 trillion years old.'

Charan smiled and said, 'Well that is why I told you that the beauty of the scriptures is that they tell you a lot about modern science and more. Let's reconcile the gaping difference of 13.7 billion vs 155.5 trillion—after all, that is thousand times differing in order of magnitude. I had cut the long story short when I said that one day of Brahma, which is called *kalpa* or aeon, has 1,000 mahayugas.

Let's look at it more granularly. One day of Brahma has 14 *manvantaras*. Manvantara means the duration for which one *manu* lives. Manu is the progenitor of the mankind. Manu is created by Brahma and Brahma himself is created by Vishnu. One manvantara has 71 mahayugas. At the end of each manvantara, comes *sandhya* which is essentially a period of localized mini-destruction. It is described as the time when *bhuloka* (or earthly planetary systems) is submerged for four Kaliyuga duration. At the end of this period, the previous Manu dies and is replaced by a new Manu who again reigns for 71 mahayugas before the next sandhya comes. This process repeats 14 times in one day of Brahma. Thus in all, there are 14 manvantaras and 15 sandhyas in one day of Brahma. If you do some math you will see that this adds up to 10,000 Kaliyugas or 1,000 mahayugas (71*10*14 + 15*4 Kaliyuga duration). Each night, as Brahma sleeps for 1,000 mahayugas, the universe is annihilated and each day, as Brahma is awake for 1,000 mahayugas, the universe is restored. A 1,000 mahayugas work out to 4.32 billion years (1000*4.3 million years). In summary, during sandhya, the Bhuloka submerges; the universe is annihilated in the night of Brahma and completely destroyed when Brahma dies.

Now, let me come to your question of 13.7 billion years being the estimated age of the universe as per the 'Lambda cold dark matter' model of the universe. Modern science estimates the age of the Sun to be 4.6 billion years and that of the Earth to be 4.5 billion years. This is erringly close to the duration of one day of Brahma which is 4.32 billion years. The age of the universe itself is estimated to be roughly three times that of the Sun and is 13.7 billion years. Bear in mind that all these dates are estimates. Science is evidence-based and it won't surprise me at all if the age of the Earth, the Sun or the universe is revised up or down with new discoveries. At any rate, what are we actually measuring when we say that the age of the universe is 13.7 billion years? Are we measuring all the cycles of annihilation and restoration that have happened thus far or only the time since the last restoration (called the Big Bang in Physics)? Even a high school student knows that we are just measuring the time since the last Big Bang.

What is interesting is that while science only talks of the Big Bang (akin to one day of Brahma) and speculates about the Big Crunch (akin to one night of Brahma), Shrimad Bhagavatam categorically mentions that this cycle continues repeatedly for 311 trillion years. Since Brahma lives for 100 years and each year has 360 days, the cycle is repeated 36,000 times with 18,000 repetitions already over! At the end of 311 trillion years, the universe will be fully destroyed and become unmanifested with Brahma himself dying.'

1 day of Brahma

	Frequency	Duration (In Kaliyuga Terms)	Total
Manvantara	14	710	9940
Sandhya	15	4	60
		Total	10,000 Kaliyuga Duration or 1,000 Mahayuga Duration

One day of Brahma

I was admiring Charan's mathematical brilliance. 'I am totally lost for words,' I said.

'And here is the final note on this. These 311 trillion years of Brahma is just one nimesa of Vishnu or smaller than a second! As Vishnu seated on the *Ananta Sheshanaag*—endless serpent in the *Kshirasagar* or the milk ocean—exhales, millions of trillions of universes emanate from the pores of Vishnu each with its own Brahma. As Vishnu inhales, those millions of trillions of universes get destroyed along with their Brahmas.'

'You mean there are multiple universes?' I was astounded.

'Of course! Our Brahma is *Chaturmukhi Brahma* or the four-headed Brahma but there are other Brahmas with fewer or more heads. The number of heads represents the complexity of the universe that the particular Brahma is in-charge of. Our universe with four dimensions—three dimensions of space and one of time—is relatively less complex than say some other universe having 11 dimensions.'

'It is only in AD 1905, which is about a 100 years ago, that Einstein came up with his theory of relativity establishing time as a dimension. How did scriptures have such detailed understanding of time many centuries ago?' I asked.

'The scriptures present a very good explanation of time and space. For example, the number 108 is considered sacred in Vedic culture. It seems erringly coincidental that the distance between the Sun and the Earth is 108 Suns and that between the Moon and the Earth is 108 Moons. What more, the size of the Sun is 108 times the size of the Earth! Shrimad Bhagavatam in Canto 9, Chapter 3 talks about the relativity of time too. One king named Kakudmi goes from the earth to Brahmaloka—the abode of Brahma—and stays there only for one muhurta or 48 minutes but is informed by Brahma that in those 48 minutes, 27 mahayugas passed on the earth. As we saw earlier, 100 years of Brahma is equal to 311 trillion years on Earth,' Charan explained.

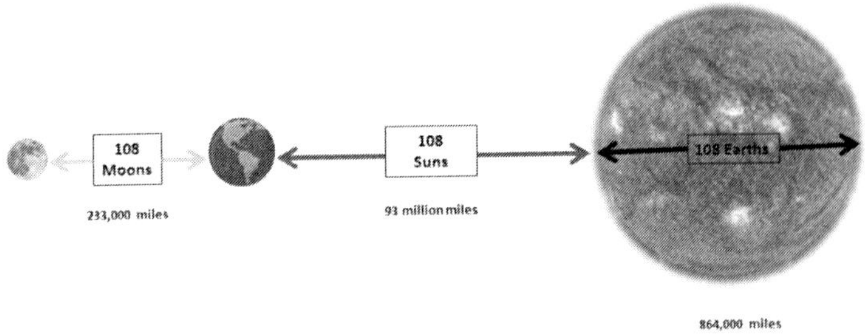

Significance of Number 108

'Time is indeed an interesting concept. It is especially interesting how it moves differently at different places depending on gravitational pull. But where exactly are we in time cycle? I remember you saying that we are in the middle of the Brahma's life cycle,' I asked.

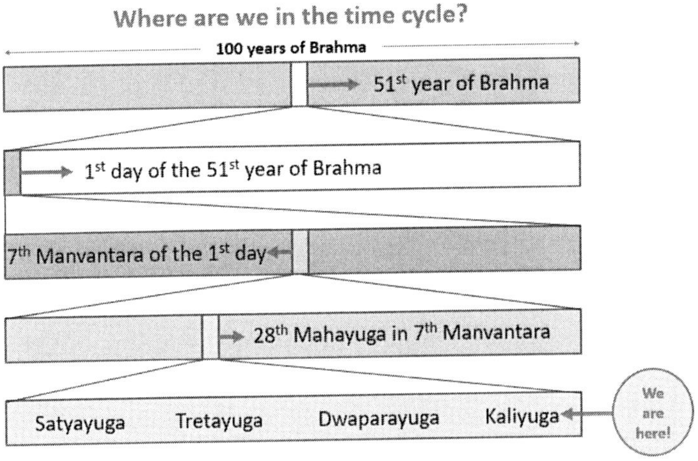

Where we are in time?

'So, if you assume Brahma to live 100 years then he just completed his 50 years yesterday and today is the first day of his fifty-first year, around noon time. The exact time being that of Kaliyuga of the twenty-eighth mahayuga cycle of the seventh manvantara. About 5,122 years of the 432,000 years of Kaliyuga have passed so far, which began at 2.27.30 a.m. on 18 February 3102 BC after Krishna left the earth.'

'Even Krishna's departure from the earth is recorded. Wow! And what about Rama?' I exclaimed.

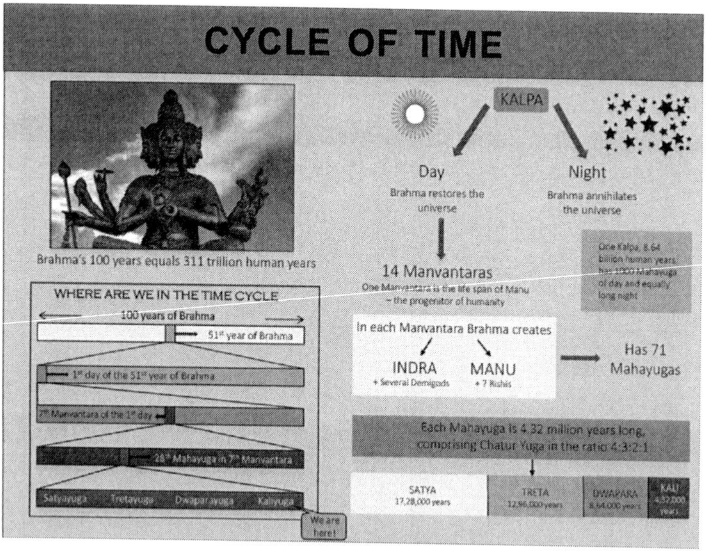

'That is also recorded. Rama came in Tretayuga but not the one which was immediately before the Dwaparayuga in which Krishna came. He came in the Tretayuga of the twenty-fourth cycle, which means that he came 4.2 mahayugas earlier which is more than 18 million years ago.'

'Eighteen million years ago!' I exhaled. But then I got back to my senses and said, 'Again this doesn't make sense because science estimates that homo sapiens only evolved 3,00,000 years ago and first life on the Earth appeared 3.8 billion years ago and the Earth is 4.5 billion years old!'

"I am glad you asked. And while we are at it, let me also add that science estimates that the Himalayas began to form approximately 50 million years ago when the Indian tectonic plate hit the Eurasian tectonic plate. But the scriptures mention the Himalayas even in the previous manvantara from an era that seems to be much older than 50 million years. As I have mentioned to you earlier, numbers such as the age of homo sapiens or the birth of the Himalayas are highly speculative. When I was in school, I learned that the age of homo sapiens is 2,00,000 years. By the time you were in school, another 1,00,000 were added to that number to make it 3,00,000 years. As and when we get more evidence, the scientific dates will continue to be revised.'

'And the scientists who come up with new findings will probably earn some good karma,' I chipped in.

With his characteristic smile, Charan said, 'Ah the good karma. How can we forget that!'

THE LAWS OF KARMA

'Who wouldn't want good karma?' I asked innocently.

'I don't!' Charan stunned me with his response.

'What do you mean? Don't we all aspire to get good karma so that it comes back to us as good fortune?' I wondered.

'No matter how much good fortune you accumulate you can never escape the four miseries which I mentioned to you earlier—birth, old age, diseases and finally death. The soul continues with this cycle or samsara over and over again endlessly until it gets liberation from this cycle,' Charan responded.

'And how does the soul get liberation?' I asked.

Charan explained, 'The soul is spiritual in nature and its destination is the spiritual world. In the material world, its journey is governed by the laws of karma. As I mentioned to you earlier, soul is actually an alien in this material world. It doesn't belong here. But whilst in the material world, it needs a body to function. The Bhagavad Gita (Verse 2.13) mentions that embodied soul continuously passes from boyhood to youth to old age and into another body at death. The Verse 2.22 further expounds that as a person puts on new garments, giving up old ones, the soul similarly accepts new material bodies, giving up the old and useless ones. In the material world, the soul is in constant need of a body. Moksha is nothing but cessation of this need.'

'And why can't soul just leave the body and go to the spiritual world and get liberated?' I questioned.

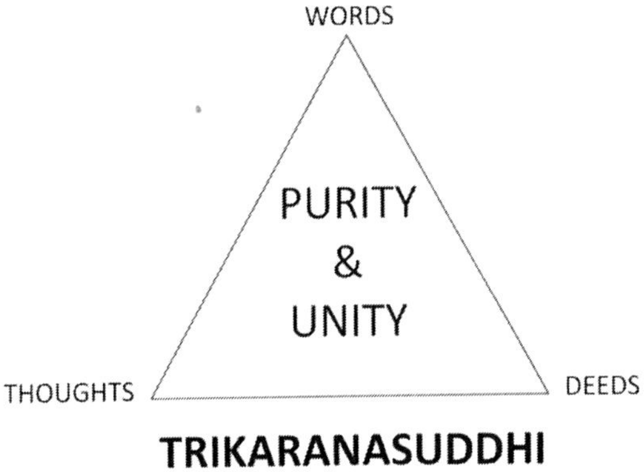

Unity of thoughts, words and deeds

'Because of the laws of karma. The journey of soul in the material world is actually very simple—governed by just one thing, karma. When the soul enters the material world, its karma score, or more precisely its *sanchit karma* meaning accumulated karma, is zero. All that soul needs to do is to make this sanchit karma score zero again so that it can get liberated. But while the rule of the game is very simple, playing it is extremely hard. Krishna acknowledges this in the Bhagavad Gita Verse 4.17, "The intricacies of karma are very hard to understand. Therefore, one should know properly what action is, what forbidden action is and what inaction is."

Even the simplest of the acts or *kriyas* create karma—breathing, eating or sleeping included. This is referred to as *kriyamana karma* meaning karma which is created due to activities or kriyas. And not just actions but even thinking accompanying the action affects karma and so does speech. In the Bhagavad Gita verses 18.14-18.15, Krishna mentions that all activities, whether good or bad, performed by a human through the body, mind or speech have five factors that influence the results of the action. Thus, contrary to the popular belief the law of karma doesn't just apply to what we do using our body but also to what we think using our mind and say through our speech. One is not separate from the other. The purity and unity of thoughts, words and deeds are referred to as *trikaranasuddhi.* It may be summarized as "talk your thought, walk your talk".

The five factors that affect the fruits of action are listed as—the physical platform (the body), the doer (the ego), the instruments (organs), the endeavour and the divine. The first factor is *adhisthanam* or the physical body which is the pedestal of desires, hatred, happiness, misery, knowledge and the like. The next is *karta* or doer which is defined as the delusional view of the individual taking the credit of the execution. The third is *karanam* or instruments which include the five knowledge organs (eyes, ears, nose, tongue and skin), five action organs (hands, legs, voice, anus and genitals), the mind and intelligence. The fourth factor is different types of *chestha* or endeavours which include various efforts. And finally, as the saying goes man proposes and god disposes, the last one is divine will.

All karma, whether good or bad, must be expended before the soul can go to the spiritual world. Both good karma and bad karma create bondage tying us to this material world. Therefore, neither good karma nor bad karma is desirable. While good karma makes life slightly easier and is akin to golden chain and bad karma makes life slightly difficult and is akin to iron chain, nonetheless, both are chains that bind us to this material world which is not our true home. Soul can't just leave the body, go to the spiritual world and get liberated as long as the chains of karma bind it.'

'How do we get rid of this chain?' I asked.

'The only way is by bringing sanchit karma to zero. The Bhagavad Gita is nothing but an explanation of how jiva interacts with prakriti in kala governed by the laws of karma designed by Ishvara or Supreme Controller. There are many temptations in this material world that keep the soul engaged in karma propelling samsara or never-ending cycles of birth and death.

The four forces of fear (*bhaya*), hope (*asha*), duty (*kartavya*) and love (*sneha*) keep us engaged in the worldly activities just as in Physics, we have four fundamental forces i.e., gravitation, electromagnetic, weak nuclear force and strong nuclear force which keep the material world together. The strongest among these is strong nuclear force, which is approximately 137 times as strong as electromagnetism, a million times as strong as the weak nuclear force and 100 undecillion times (or 100 trillion trillion trillion times) as strong as gravitational force.

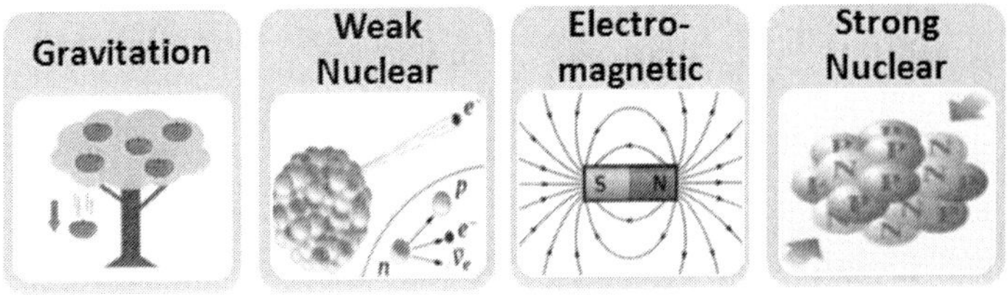

The four fundamental forces of nature

Fear or bhaya stems from the need for self-preservation. Every human is concerned with self-preservation. The question is existential. Fear can often make us swallow the bitter pill when presented with an uncomfortable choice. Countries spend billions of dollars in fear that they may be attacked. Since time immemorial political leaders have used fear both as a means of control and as a tool to access power. Fear is the fundamental force driving most people. Most of our actions are a result of fear—fear of a tyrant ruler, fear of law, fear of losing out or even fear of dying. Like gravity, it is the most observable force. But it is also the weakest.

Hope or asha stems from aspiration. Every human is concerned with aspiration. Hope is the force that keeps us going in adversity. "This too shall pass" is a hope. In Greek mythology, when Pandora, the first woman on earth, let out evils by opening the box the only solace was the Hope Fairy. Hope gives resilience to us as individuals and also as mankind. Without hope, all pursuits come to an end. Hope can make you move past fear. Overcoming their fear, thousands of people cross the North Korean border or cross the Mediterranean from Syria to Europe in hope of a better life.

Hope, stemming from aspirations, can lead to desires which when taken to an extreme can result in greed or lust. The Bhagavad Gita (verses 2.62 and 2.63) explain, "When one thinks of the objects, attachment to the object arises; from attachments, desire is born; from desire, anger rises; from anger, comes delusion; from delusion, the loss of memory; from loss of memory, the destruction of discrimination; from destruction of discrimination, one perishes." Hopes, desires and aspirations are innate to us all but we seldom accept or admit them openly. Unlike fear, hope is not always visible to the naked eye, but lurking, nevertheless. Hidden within us, hope is akin to weak nuclear force which is always there but unlike gravity is not openly visible.

Duty or kartavya comes from the sense of righteousness. Most humans are righteous. We want to do the right thing. We often confuse duty with fear or love but it is neither of them. Duty is an independent concept. Loosely speaking, duty is the right thing to do. It is a very strong force as most of us want to be morally right always. When a sense of duty arises, fears get annihilated and desires wane away. Duty cannot be induced on its own. Duty towards whom? Duty for what? Just like iron behaves like magnet in presence of electromagnetic fields, duty also needs a focal point to manifest. For example, duty towards one's country, duty to mankind, and so on. Hence duty is akin to electromagnetic forces.

Finally, we have love or sneha. Love stems from the sense of selflessness. How can any discussion on human forces be complete without love? Love is completely selfless. Anything which is not selfless is probably not love. Love is the most potent force on the planet. It is much more powerful than fear, desire and duty put together. Love is akin to strong nuclear force. Strong nuclear force is the strongest force in nature and is responsible for keeping the nucleus of atoms together. Without this force, the atoms will disintegrate. What would happen without love? Well, humanity will disintegrate!

The four fundamental forces that keep us engaged in worldly activities

The Bhagavad Gita tells us how to play this game of karma such that we get liberated from these strong forces. It tells that one must aim for *akarma* and not good karma.'

'Akarma?' I asked with a puzzled look.

'Akarma is a state where actions or kriyas do not accrue kriyamana karma—hence there is no addition or deduction in the sanchit karma balance. While there is no new addition or deletion, whatever sanchit karma the soul has already accumulated still needs to be spent before liberation can happen. This fructification of karma is referred to as destiny or *prarabdha karma.* So if you were to compare karma to a bank account then sanchit karma is like wealth, i.e., the total money in the bank, kriyamana karma is salary, i.e., whatever new money you keep adding to the bank account, and prarabdha karma is like the expenditure, i.e., whatever money you take out from the bank. In the beginning your bank balance is zero and you are liberated when the bank balance is zero again. So the aim of life should be to aspire for *akarma,* i.e., to do *kriyas* or actions in such a way that they do not add to your karma balance. Only then will you get liberated; otherwise you will keep adding new karma and never get liberated.'

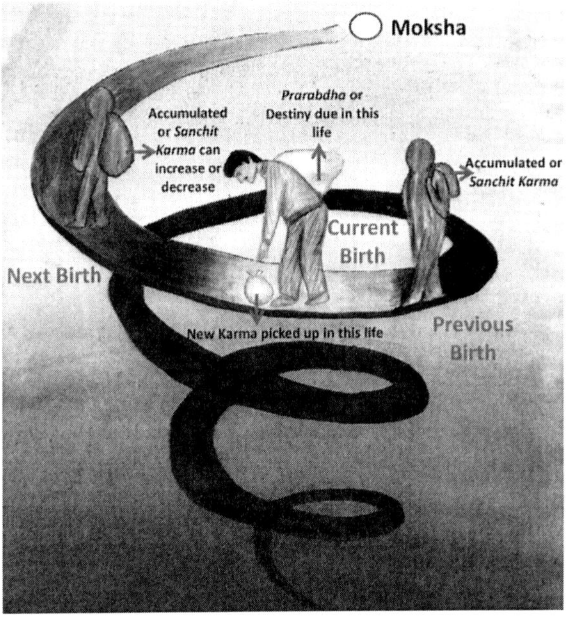

Different types of karma

The Karma Equation

$$Sanchit_i = Sanchit_{i-1} - Prarabdha_i + Kriyamana_i$$

where

$Sanchit_i$ is accumulated karma at the end of current life
$Sanchit_{i-1}$ is accumulated karma at the end of previous life
$Prarabdha_i$ is that portion of *Sanchit karma* which is due as destiny in current life
$Kriyamana_i$ is new karma which one accumulates in current life through *kriyas*

Sanchit Karma – **Wealth**
Parabhdha Karma – **Expense**
Kriyamana Karma – **Salary**

Kriya vs Karma

Karma ≠ Duty!

- Sanchit Karma – Your current bank Balance
- Parabhdha Karma – That whose fruits are due in this life time (Destiny)
- Kriyamana Karma – What you are adding to your bank account right now

'I am so surprised. All my life I thought one must do good karma and today you have flipped that concept totally on its head!' I reflected.

'Actually, karma is in fact the most popular and unfortunately also the most misunderstood concept of the Bhagavad Gita. As Einstein says things should be made as simple as possible, but no simpler. Karma is a classic case of Occam's Razor taken too far and as a result the modern world has some really perverted and convoluted interpretation of karma. People have even come up with the theories that even animals accumulate karma.'

'You mean they don't?' I asked surprised.

'No, they don't. As per scriptures, there are 8.4 million species with various levels of consciousness. Unlike in biology, these 8.4 million species are arranged on the basis of their consciousness and not by phenotype or genotype. Only the 0.4 million human-like species accrue karma and the rest 8 million don't because only these 0.4 million species are conscious enough to have a choice of action. Where there is no choice, there is no karma since those species act simply on the basis of instincts. As the movie Spiderman says, "With great power comes great responsibility."

When superior consciousness is granted to the soul then it is expected to act responsibly. Padma Purana mentions:

jalajā nava-lakṣāṇi
sthāvarā lakṣa-viṁśati
kṛmayo rudra-saṅkhyakāḥ
pakṣiṇāṁ daśa-lakṣaṇam
triṁśal-lakṣāṇi paśavaḥ
catur-lakṣāṇi mānuṣāḥ

It means that there are two million immobile life forms such as plants and trees, 0.9 million water-based forms of life such as fish, 1.1 million reptiles, one million birds, three million terrestrial animals and finally 0.4 million human-like species. Modern human or homo sapiens falls in these 0.4 million human-like species and so do demigods, including Brahma, the creator of the universe, and Indra, the lord of demigods. There are 33 primary demigods or Vedic deities and 330 million minor demigods. The 33 primary demigods are in-charge of various aspects of nature and are sons of sage Kashyapa and Aditi who is defined as viśve devā or the Universal Deity who is *aditirjātamaditirjanitvam*—all that has been and will be—in Rig Veda (Verse 1.89.10). Her 33 sons are 12 Adityas, 11 Rudras, eight Vasus and two Ashvinis. Among others, they include the sun god, Vivasvan; the ocean god, Varuna; the fortune god, Bhaga; the god of desire, Kama; the fire god, Agni; the Earth god, Prithvi; the god of winds, Vayu and the Moon god, Chandra.

33 VEDIC DEITIES
(Adityas, Rudras, Vasus, Ashvins)

12 Adityas	11 Rudras	8 Vasus
Vivasvān	Raivata	Prithvi (Earth)
Aryamā	Aja	Āpa (Water)
Pūṣā	Bhava	Agni (Fire)
Tvaṣṭā	Bhīma	Vāyu (Wind)
Savitā	Vāma	Akasha (Sky)
Bhaga	Ugra	Pratyūsha (Sun)
Dhātā	Vṛṣākapi	Chandrama (Moon)
Vidhātā	Ajaikapāt	Nakstrani (Stars)
Varuṇa	Ahirbradhna	
Mitra	Bahurūpa	
Śatru	Mahān	**2 Ashvins**
Urukrama		

In all these life forms, from a tiny ant to the mighty demigods, soul is the only constant while the body keeps changing. You could be a mosquito, then a rat, then a lion, then Indra and so on. Governed by the laws of karma, souls keep moving up and down these 8.4 million possibilities—these 8.4 million species themselves are composed of varying permutations and combinations of the three fundamental modes or gunas of sattva, rajas and tamas.

Just like the three primary colour pixels of red, green and blue can produce millions of hues on a phone screen, the three modes of sattva, rajas and tamas can produce millions of species. Depending on what karma and desires the soul has at the moment of death, it can get the next body from that of the mighty Indra (the lord of demigods) to a tiny ant. Life is nothing but a preparation for death. The desires at death are not different from the life one has been living all along. If one has been pious all life then the desires at death are *sattvic*. If one has been evil all life then the desires at death are *tamasic*. Death is the final test. One gets whole life to prepare for this test. Hence one must prepare well.

While you may have the desire to get a really expensive designer suit, without enough money in the pocket, you can't afford it. Similarly, you might desire to be Indra but if you don't have enough karma points then you can't afford to attain the position of Indra. Karma is indeed the price a soul pays for purchasing a new body. The 8.4 million species represent nothing but the 8.4 million types of body choices available to the soul. It is like a key fitting into a lock. The body is the lock and soul's desire is the key. The different shapes and sizes of the key are formed by varying combinations of the three modes of sattva, rajas and tamas. If the desire is to devour meat all the time then a lion's body is assigned. If the desire is to be static then there is a body of a tree to that effect. If the desire is to sleep all the time then a bear's body is given. For each combination of desires, there is an appropriate body available. The key must not only fit the right lock but also needs the right twisting force to open the lock. Karma points are the force needed to twist the key and open the lock.

While narrating a story to the eldest of the Pandavas, Yudhishthira, in the 'Vana Parva' section of the Mahabharata, Sage Markandeya mentions:

śubhaiḥ prayogair devatvaṁ vyāmiśrair mānuṣo bhavet |
mohanīyair viyonīśu tvadhogāmī ca kilbiṣaiḥ ||
jāti mṛtyu jarā duḥkhaiḥ satataṁ samabhidrutaḥ |
saṁsāre pacyamānaśca doṣair ātma kṛtair naraḥ ||
tiryag yoni sahasrāṇi gatvā narakam eva ca |
jīvāḥ saṁparivartante karma bandha nibandhanāḥ ||
tataḥ karma samādatte punar anyan navaṁ bahu |
pacyate tu punas tena bhuktvā'pathyam ivāturaḥ ||

It means, "By the performance of virtuous actions, one attains the state of the gods, and by a combination of good and evil, one acquires a human birth; by indulgence in rank sensuality and similar demoralizing practices, one is born in the lower species of animals, and by deplorable acts, one goes to the infernal regions. Because of the consequences of their own actions, jīvas are subjected to the miseries of birth, old age and death. People are repeatedly born and die and are metamorphosed here in samsara. Passing through thousands of animal births and also the infernal regions, the jivas wander about, secured by the bonds of their own karma. In the human birth, they accumulate a new series of karma, and they consequently continue to suffer misery, like sick people partaking of unwholesome food,' Charan gave a detailed explanation of how karma works.

I responded, 'I am amazed that the scriptures talk about plants as species. It was only in 1901 that the famous Indian scientist and inventor of wireless transmission Jagdish Chandra Bose proved that plants have life. I totally agree that if animals have no control over their actions then they should not bear the consequences of their actions and hence should not accrue karma. But how does karma work for humans? And can humans become animals or trees again? Is that also determined by karma?'

'Human-like life form is very precious as only in this state of consciousness can the soul get liberated. Human-like life is the junction from where one could go to heaven (*svarga*) or hell (*naraka*) or come back to this earth as a human or an animal or a plant or even get out of this material world and reach the spiritual world. As mentioned earlier, the remaining eight million life forms do not accumulate karma. They are just spending time without incurring any karma. A tiger can kill five deers in a day and that has no bearing on its karma. On the other hand, for humans, even the simple act of eating has repercussions on karma notwithstanding the fact that without eating humans will die! In order to keep themselves alive, humans have to invariably kill some forms of plants and animals.

Thus, even the most basic act of keeping the body alive triggers massive chains of karmic reactions for humans. The aim of human-like life form is to realize the potential of being able to spend all karma, accumulate no new karma and move towards moksha. Most humans do not make good use of this privilege and continue living more like a two-legged animal indulging only in sleeping, eating, entertaining and defending rather than thinking of the higher purpose of *Athato Brahma Jigyasa*. Such individuals are at the risk of getting demoted to a lower life form of an animal or a tree since they did not make use of the human body they were granted.

Within us we have the power of becoming mighty Indra, the lord of demigods, or a tiny ant. It all depends on how we act and what karma we accumulate. Given enough good karma, anyone can become Indra. There is a beautiful story in the Brahma Vaivarta Purana titled 'Indra and the Ant' where a Brahmin boy in the middle of a talk with Indra sees an army of ants passing by. The boy chuckles and says, "These ants are all former Indras. Through laws of karma across many lifetimes they rise from lowest consciousness to the highest illumination of being—Indra—and when pride fills them down they go. It is by laws of karma that one attains the position of a Brahmin or Indra or Brahma or acquires happiness or sorrow. It is through laws of karma that one becomes a master or a servant, acquires beauty or deformity, or is reborn as a monster."'

'But you said that accumulating good karma is not the goal of soul. Why does then one need good karma to become Indra?' I asked.

'No, it is not the goal of the soul. The very next line in the Brahma Vaivarta Purana says, "In this universe with the combination of time, death hovers around the head of everyone. Everything of the creatures irrespective of good and bad is like the water bubbles." Even the powerful Indra is subject to the misery of death. Twenty-eight Indras are replaced in one day and night of Brahma and Brahma himself dies in 311 trillion years. The goal of life is to get liberation from this cycle of birth and death and go to the spiritual world.

The soul is *sat, chit, ananda,* meaning eternal, superconscious and blissful. But it realizes this only when it is in the spiritual world or vaikuntha. In vaikuntha, the soul is called a "liberated soul"—free from a body. When the soul comes to the material world, it acquires a subtle and/or a gross body and becomes an "embodied soul". An embodied soul is a conditioned soul—conditioned by the body it encases itself in. The conditioned soul sees the world through this layer of body much the same way as someone looking at the world from a tainted glass. One's worldview gets coloured due to the colour of the glass. This tainted worldview is called maya or illusion.

The soul is marginal energy or *tatastha shakti* capable of existing in both the spiritual universe or internal energy (*antaranga shakti*) as well as material universe or external energy (*bahiranga shakti*). Antaranga shakti manifests as the spiritual world, bahiranga shakti manifests as the material world and in-between those two are jivas which are called tatastha shakti, or marginal energy, because they are at liberty to live in either external or internal energy. Jivas living within the spiritual world are called liberated souls, whereas the residents of the external world are called the conditioned souls.

The living entities have spiritual qualities of *satchitananda* where sat means eternal, chit means superconscious and ananda means blissful. If the spiritual world is like fire then jivas are akin to sparks—having the same qualities as the fire and in fact originating from the fire yet different. This spark can either go astray in the material world or go back to the spiritual fire it came from.

The spiritual universe has spiritual planets called vaikunthas while the material universe has material planetary systems. Imagine the universe with a 46-billion-light-year radius and beyond. There are billions and billions of such universes each coming out from the pores of Vishnu each with its own Brahma. All these billions and billions of universes are just one-fourth of the creation. The rest three-fourth is spiritual. Our own universe or Brahmanda or literally the egg of Brahma—the four-headed god of our universe—has 14 layers of planetary systems called *lokas* and 28 types of hells called narakas. These lokas are gradation from sattva to tamas with satyaloka having the highest sattva quotient and narakas having the highest tamas quotient.

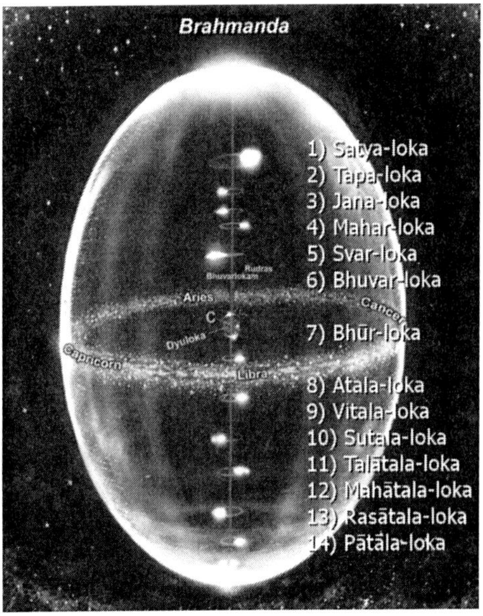

14 lokas

The 14 lokas are *satya, tapa, jana, mahar, svar or svarga, bhuvar, bhur, atala, vitala, sutala, talatala, mahatala, rasatala* and *patala*. Each of these lokas or planetary systems has billions and billions of planets within them. The first six are called higher planetary systems and the last seven are called lower planetary systems. The Earth belongs to the middle planetary system called *bhurloka* as do other planets such as Jupiter, Saturn, Mercury, etc. Lord Brahma lives in the highest planetary system of satyaloka and demigods led by Indra dwell in the heavenly planets—*svargaloka*.

Beneath these 14 planetary systems are hellish planets of narakas. They lie below the *patalaloka*. Twenty-eight different types of hells are described in the *Shrimad Bhagvatam* Verse 5.26.7—*tāmisra, andhatāmisra, raurava, mahāraurava, kumbhīpāka, kālasūtra, asipatravana, sūkaramukha, andhakūpa, kṛmibhojana, sandaṁśa, taptasūrmi, vajrakaṇṭaka-śālmalī, vaitaraṇī, pūyoda, prāṇarodha, viśasana, lālābhakṣa, sārameyādana, avīci, ayaḥpāna, kṣārakardama, rakṣogaṇa-bhojana, śūlaprota, dandaśūka, avaṭa-nirodhana, paryāvartana* and *sūcīmukha*.

The gunas of sattva, rajas and tamas operate in the material world. The spiritual world is free from the influence of gunas. The spiritual world is over and beyond the gunas. Tatastha shakti (jiva) looks at the material world and gets curious about it. This curiosity is the root cause of soul coming to the material plane. In the material world, the soul needs a body—subtle and/or gross. It can go up or down various lokas and narakas depending on the karma it accumulates in the material world. The cycle of life and death is fueled by the karma of the soul. Unless all the karma is burnt out, the soul will keep travelling up and down these 14 lokas and 28 narakas.

In all these planetary systems, the soul needs a material body. For example, in bhurloka where the earth is situated, the soul needs both gross body made up of panchamahabhuta as well as subtle body comprising mind, intelligence and ahamkaara. In the svargaloka, the soul only needs a subtle body i.e., mind, intelligence and ahamkaara. Usually, gross body is not allowed in svargaloka. Have you ever seen anyone depart from the earth with their gross body? However, the Mahabharata mentions that the eldest Pandava, Yudhishthira, was so pure that he landed in svargaloka with his gross mortal body. The Pandavas spent some time in naraka for the small sins they committed before they went to svargaloka. But even in this svargaloka ruled by demigod Indra, happiness is ephemeral having a clear beginning and an end. A fully realized soul knows this and aims at the true bliss of vaikuntha rather than the momentary happiness of svarga.

In the Bhagavad Gita (Verse 8.16), Krishna tells Arjuna, "From the highest planet in the material world down to the lowest, all are places of misery wherein repeated birth and death take place. But one who attains to My abode, never takes birth again." Having said this, Anveshak, know that Indra is a very high post for a jiva. As I mentioned to you both good karma and bad karma need to be expended before a jiva gets liberated. A jiva which has accumulated enough good karma can actually aspire to become Indra. However, such a soul would be considered a misguided soul if it aims to become Indra to enjoy the opulences of svarga as svarga itself is not eternal. Even Indra must die and svarga itself gets annihilated during pralaya. Similarly, there are many misguided humans on Earth who keep doing good deeds or *punya* in the hope of reaping its benefits in the form of good luck.'

'So one should not do good deeds?' I asked perplexed.

'Of course, one should do good deeds. But one should do it without any desire. When a good deed is done with an expectation of a reward then it accumulates good karma but when the same good deed is done without any selfish desire, i.e., *nishkama karma*, then it becomes *akarma*, i.e., it accumulates no karma. Thus, the same act can be liberating or binding depending on one's consciousness. A realized soul executes its duties without expecting anything in return whereas an unrealized soul is in the mode of indulgence constantly counting the benefits of good deeds it does. Every act can possibly be *sukarma* (good karma), *vikarma* (bad karma) or akarma (neutral karma). What do you think charity is: sukarma, vikarma or akarma?'

'Charity is a good thing. So, it should be sukarma, right?' I responded.

'Not necessarily. As I said it depends on the consciousness or mode in which the charity was done. When the charity is done with the expectation that the next day the whole town knows about it and your name comes on the first page of the newspaper then it is merely a good deed or sukarma. But when the same act of charity is done with no expectations then it becomes akarma. So, you see our thinking or mindset is as important as doing when it comes to how karma works. And perhaps what may surprise you is that the same act of charity can potentially be vikarma or bad karma. Let's say the charity money you gave was later used for say terrorism or religious persecution then it will get you bad karma.'

'But how is that fair? How would I know what the money I gave for charity is used for? I donated in good faith,' I was bewildered.

'Anveshak, you can't be absolved of your responsibilities by pleading ignorance. Let's say a cloth manufacturer retailer in Europe outsources its manufacturing to countries with lower production costs. It is later found out that the outsourced companies use child labour in their factories. Do you think the European retailer is responsible?'

'I think the European retailer should have done adequate research on his part,' I responded.

'So the same thing applies to individuals as well, Anveshak. We should take full cognizance of our actions or we risk even the best of our intentions turning against us and resulting in bad karma.'

'I understand that we can unknowingly get bad karma but why do bad things happen to good people?' I asked confused.

'One is often perplexed to see bad things happen to good people. We often notice nice people getting cancer or even worse, babies born without limbs or eyes. One wonders why this has happened and there seems to be no justification. The journey of a soul is very long. What one is looking at is but an instantaneous snapshot of a very long movie. Imagine a tank filled with liquids of different colours stacked one on top of the other. When you open the tap, you see red liquid coming out and you are perplexed how red liquid is coming out when blue is being poured from the top. Karma works similarly. What you see today is the outcome of what was put in a long time back, potentially across many lives. What is being put today will manifest its results sometime in future—maybe in this lifetime or in future lives. We understand this as destiny. Yes, one may be destined to certain things in life, blindness and cancer included, but that is not independent of one's karma. In fact, destiny is nothing but fructification of past karma as *prarabdha* or providence.'

'Sometimes it is so hard to resist doing bad deeds or *paap*. Why do we sometimes do bad deeds even if we know it is wrong?" I continued my query.

'In the Bhagavad Gita (Verse 3.36), Arjuna asks Krishna the same question, "What impels one to sinful acts, even unwillingly, as if engaged by force?" In the next few verses, Krishna explains the power of guna to Arjuna and mentions, "It is lust only, Arjuna, which is born because of contact with the material mode or guna of passion and later transformed into wrath, and which is the all-devouring sinful enemy of this world. As fire is covered by smoke, as a mirror is covered by dust, or as the embryo is covered by the womb, the living entity is similarly covered by different degrees of this lust. Thus, the wise living entity's pure consciousness gets covered by its eternal enemy in the form of lust, which is never satisfied, and which burns like fire. The senses, the mind and the intelligence are the sitting places of this lust. Through them, lust covers the real knowledge of the living entity and bewilders him. Therefore, O Arjuna, in the very beginning curb this great symbol of sin (lust) by regulating the senses and slay this destroyer of knowledge and self-realization."'

'So, if sometimes we do good activities and sometimes we do bad things, will the paap and punya cancel out each other?' I probed deeper.

Charan smiled, 'If you sow five sweet mango seeds and three sour lemon seeds then do you get only two mango trees because the three sour lemons cancel out the sweet mangoes? You will get fruits of both. Similarly, one needs to bear the fruits of all good and bad deeds one has done. They don't cancel out the effects of each other. However, as I have mentioned to you, one should not worry about calculating paap and punya, but rather focus on doing one's duty and perfecting akarma. Overthinking the consequences of one's deeds is only likely to confuse a person. It is better to focus on nishkama karma. Under ordinary circumstances, usually killing is bad and will result in vikarma or bad karma but Arjuna, who killed thousands in the Mahabharata war, did not get any paap for his deeds because he was not killing for his pleasure or self-gratification, but for selfless duty of establishing dharma. Such killing is akarmic. If Arjuna started to calculate his paap and punya in the war, then he would have had no time to perform his duty. Therefore, focus on your purpose in life and not on mathematics of paap and punya.'

'I think they were destined to die,' I said nonchalantly.

Charan corrected me, 'Actually, destiny is in our hands. Everything happening now had a cause in the past. Everything you do now will have a reaction in the future. This is how karma works. If you are sitting in a plane which is bound for London, you may say the plane is destined to go to London and you have no control over it but actually at one point you had a choice whether to board that plane or not. Destiny works the same way. Many times, it feels we have no control over our destiny but actually what constitutes destiny today is a result of actions we had taken in the past. Moreover, you may notice that sometimes unfortunately the plane crashes with no survivors. One wonders how it is that everyone coming from such diverse backgrounds, of different ages and belonging to different countries met the same fate. This is called collective karma. Through some mechanism of past actions, they all happen to come together and meet the same fate. Likewise, sometimes for no reason, some good things happen to us. This is called *agyat sukriti*. We may have unknowingly done some good deeds in the past and they fructify in the form of good luck for no apparent reason.'

'Indeed, nature has strange ways,' I reflected.

WHO IS GOD?

Acknowledging my assertion Charan said, 'Nature indeed has strange ways. As they say, it is impossible to understand the ways of God with the mind of a human.'

'And who is God?' I probed.

Charan started to unbundle the puzzle, 'It is impossible to trap the concept of God in any noun, verb or adjective or even mathematics or physics that mankind is capable of. We can logically conclude that the perfect, infinite God cannot possibly be understood by our limited, illusion-ridden, inaccurate and inexperienced senses. On an intellectual level, it would be like trying to explain quantum physics to a dog that typically has an IQ of 30 and capture it in the form of dog's barks. The wonders of the universe are too wide and vast to be interpretable to even the most intelligent among us who hardly hit an IQ of 230 at best. Even with our best IQ, there is a limit to what we can know. But even if we were not limited by IQ, there are several reasons why we still can't make sense of the universe. I had already explained to you how we can never get any information about what lies beyond a 46-billion-light-year radius because those galaxies are moving away from us faster than light (or any information) can travel. This puts limitations of Physics on why we can't make sense of the universe—if we can't even observe how big the universe is, how can we ever make complete deductions about it? But let's assume that this was not a limitation and we could somehow get information from those galaxies. Can we understand the universe then?'

I thought deeply and said, 'My opinion is that if we did not have limits on our intelligence and we could get all the information there is in the universe, then using limitless intelligence we could process that information to make sense of the universe.'

Charan planted seeds of doubts in my thinking, 'That sounds plausible, and in fact, scientists believed so until Austrian logician Kurt Gödel proved that there may be a gap between truth and proof. We call our understanding of the universe as physics but laws of physics are mathematically derived. But what if that mathematics itself was incomplete and inconsistent?'

'Incomplete and inconsistent?' I asked puzzled.

Charan continued with his explanation, 'The fundamental belief in Mathematics was that if a statement is true then it can be proved until Gödel's incompleteness theorem placed a limitation on what we might be able to know even in something as fundamental as mathematics on which all physics is based.[27] Gödel demonstrated that if we begin with a series of axioms in any mathematical system, there will always be some statements that can't be proven true or false using the set of axioms we began with. You may argue in that case that this new statement itself is an axiom because by definition an axiom is something that doesn't need to be proved and is a fundamental postulate. And hence we should add this statement to the initial set of axioms and then we can prove every statement to be true or false. But even if you do so, new statements can still be created which can't be proven with this new increased set of axioms. In fact, no matter how many axioms you keep adding you will always end up with statements that cannot be proven. This effectively proved that no system of mathematical axioms is both consistent (i.e., never leading to contradictions) and complete (i.e., serving as the building blocks of all mathematical truths). The ramifications on human knowledge structure are quite important. Essentially it showed that there will always be a gap in any theory we propose—even the most fundamental ones in Mathematics—and hence there will always be "God of gaps".

I hope you can now see why I said that it is impossible to understand the ways of God with the mind of a human. An extension of Gödel's theorem is Chaitin's theorem which says that a system cannot build anything more complex than itself. By definition, we humans are a part of this very universe we are trying to understand. No matter how hard we try we can never make complete sense of the universe as we are part of the whole. It would be like the RAM of a computer trying to understand how the entire computer works when it is itself just a part of the whole computer and hence by definition is less complex than the entire computer.'

'So, there is no way to understand God?' I asked.

Charan replied, 'Even when physics and mathematics fail us, there are many words that attempt to capture the concept of God such as Brahman, Bhagavan, Paramatma or Ishvara. All of them are related terms but have subtle differences. My personal favourite is GOD—Generator, Operator and Destroyer. It sums up almost everything we attribute to God—creation, maintenance and obliteration. The same is captured in the *Trimurti* concept of God comprising Brahma, Vishnu and Mahesh where Brahma is the creator, Vishnu is the protector and Mahesh is the destroyer of the universe. In Chapter 8 of the Bhagavad Gita, Arjuna asks Krishna, "What is Brahman? What is Adhyatma?" to which Krishna responds, "The indestructible is Brahman and its essential nature or *swabhaav* is adhyatma (study of the self)." The word "Brahman"—not to be confused by the four-headed Brahma, the creator of our universe—comes from the root word "brh" which means "to swell, expand, grow, enlarge". Thus, Brahman represents big or grand and is actually quite a beautiful concept of God referring to the unique unity behind the baffling diversity in the universe. Paradoxically, He is so big that He pervades even the smallest gap in the universe. The Mundaka Upanishad (Verse 3.1.7) mentions:

> bṛhac ca tad divyam acintya-rūpaṁ sūkṣmāc ca tat sūkṣma-taraṁ vibhāti

It means "the all-pervading Brahman is of unthinkable form—larger than space and subtler than the subtlest". So, if you can imagine the smallest thing possible (which in modern scientific terms would be Planck length or 1.6 * 10^{-35} metres) then Brahman is smaller than that and if you can imagine the biggest thing possible (which in modern scientific terms would be the universe of 46 billion light years in radius) then Brahman is bigger than that! It is like the sky—everywhere yet nowhere. It is the basis of everything from micro to macro but appears to be nothing. It connotes the unchanging, permanent, all-pervasive, infinite, eternal reality in the universe—the formal and final cause of all that exists. It is everywhere and inside all beings. The Bhagavad Gita (Verse 4.24) says, "In the practice of seeing Brahman everywhere as a form of sacrifice, Brahman is the ladle (with which the oblation is poured into the fire); Brahman again is the oblation; Brahman is the fire, Brahman itself is the sacrifice, and so Brahman itself constitutes the act of pouring the oblation into the fire. And finally, Brahman is the goal to be reached by him who is absorbed in Brahman as the act of such sacrifice." Brahma Samhita (Verse 5.35) sums this up nicely:

eko 'py asau racayituṁ jagad-aṇḍa-koṭiṁ
yac-chaktir asti jagad-aṇḍa-cayā yad-antaḥ
aṇḍāntara-stha-paramāṇu-cayāntara-stham

It means, "He is an undifferentiated entity as there is no distinction between potency and its possessor. In His work of creation of millions of universes, His potency remains inseparable. All universes exist in Him and He is present in every atom scattered throughout the universes and even the space between the atoms." So as you can see, He is not just the creator but also inside all creation and yet having created so much He does not diminish. His potency remains inseparable. The Isha Upanishad mentions the same:

oṁ pūrṇam adaḥ pūrṇam idaṁ pūrṇāt pūrṇam udacyate
pūrṇasya pūrṇam ādāya pūrṇam evāvaśiṣyate

It means, "He is perfect and complete, and because he is completely perfect, all emanations from Him, such as this phenomenal world, are perfectly equipped as complete wholes. Whatever is produced of the complete whole is also complete in itself. Because He is the complete whole, even though so many complete units emanate from Him, He remains the complete balance."'

I wondered aloud, 'But how is it possible that you

create something from self and yet you remain complete as before. If I am emanating something then surely I must be diminishing. For example, the Sun emits rays and it is continuously diminishing. The mass of the Sun is forever getting converted into energy. This energy is emitted in form of light and heat. Every moment, every second, the Sun is reducing. So if God is creating millions of universes then surely He must be reducing.'

Charan responded, 'Glad you asked. You might have come across Banach-Tarski theorem in Mathematics. Essentially what it says is that if you begin with one ball, take it apart and then rearrange, you can rearrange it in such a way that you end up with two balls, both identical to the original one. So effectively you created two from just one. Those two are exactly identical in all aspects—size, volume, weight and density. Sounds like a paradox, doesn't it? How can we get double of something starting with just one? You never had a problem with that, did you?"

'Yeah but that is possible because the ball is assumed to be infinitely divisible,' I reasoned.

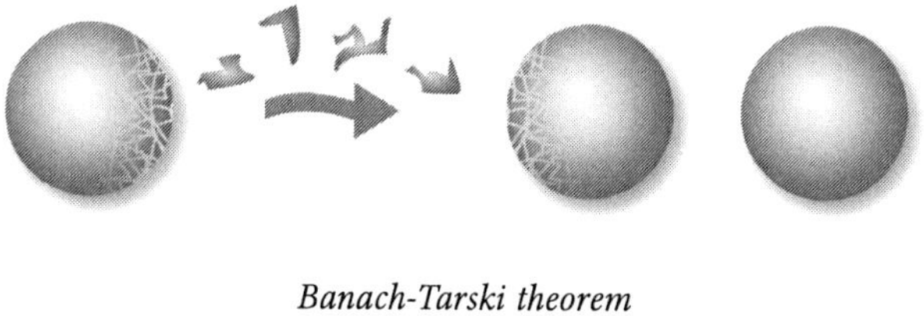

Banach-Tarski theorem

'And therein lies your answer—the logic of something diminishing when it is emitting parts of it applies to finite objects. God is infinite—whether you take out something from infinity or add something to infinity, it remains infinite.

God can create infinite numbers of infinitely big universes and yet remain infinite! As humans, we are not very great at visualizing zero and infinite. Our intuitive logic, mathematics, and physics essentially break down at singularities laden with the concepts of infinity and zero. In Physics, the primordial singularity, which we believe to be the genesis of the universe, is called 'the Big Bang' yet we know essentially nothing about this singularity—what caused it, where did it come from, what was it made of or what was there before it? These are some unanswered and very disturbing questions that science is yet to answer. We claim God is dead because science has all the answers, yet we can't even answer a simple question—where did the universe come from? It will not be an overstatement to say that science has simply reduced the 'Creator God' to the 'Creator Point', which is better known as the Big Bang.'

I reminisced, 'Now I recall that in my high school Physics classes, my teacher had mentioned that universe is nothing but a blob of energy and mass, with mass and energy being interchangeable—a rarified form of mass is energy, and condensed form of energy is mass. So all the mass in the universe can be converted to equivalent energy as per Einstein's $E=mc^2$ formula. And where there is mass there is gravity. Gravitational potential energy is negative. It is postulated that the sum total of all the negative gravitational energy totally balances out all the mass and the other energies, such as light, in the universe. Together they sum up to zero, meaning that the universe is nothing but just a big blob of zero. And the fun fact is that two times zero is also zero. So we can effectively double the amount of mass in the universe and the negative gravitational energy will increase correspondingly ensuring that everything again sums to zero. In effect, we doubled the universe without breaking any laws of Physics! I never thought of God to be infinite creating infinitely many infinitely big universes. It is a bit hard for me to visualize an infinite God.'

Charan responded, 'Understanding and appreciating infinity with our finite minds may be hard. And that is why we have other ways of trying to understand God. The Bhagavad Gita (Verse 15.15) hints at the Paramatma or the Supreme Soul concept of God—*sarvasya cāhaṁ hṛdi sanniviṣṭo*—as does the Verse 18.61, *isvarah sarva-bhutanam hrd-dese,* as well as the Verse 10.20, *sarva-bhūtāśaya-sthitaḥ.* They all mean: "I am seated in everyone's heart." The same concept is elaborated in Mundaka Upanishad (Verse 3.1.1):

dvā suparṇā sayujā sakhāyā samānaṃ
vṛkṣaṃ pariṣasvajāte
tayoranyaḥ pippalaṃ svādvattyanaśnannanyo abhicākaśīti

It means, "Two inseparable companions of fine plumage perch on the self-same tree. One of the two feeds on the delicious fruit. The other, not tasting it, looks on." If this body were a tree then both atma and Paramatma are present within—the atma is the bird that feeds on the delicious fruit of karma while the Paramatma is the bird, who simply watches. Thus, God is not only all-pervading but also localized in everyone's heart."

The Bhagavad Gita (Verse 8.9) says:

kaviṁ purāṇam anuśāsitāram aṇor aṇīyāṁsam anusmared yaḥ
sarvasya dhātāram acintya-rūpam
āditya-varṇaṁ tamasaḥ parastāt

It means, "One who knows everything, the oldest, the controller, smaller than the smallest, the maintainer of everything, of inconceivable form, luminous like the Sun and beyond the darkness (of ignorance)". This is alluding to Ishvara concept of God which means one with great capabilities or the great controller. We are all controllers in some sense—able to control some things, but not everything. Hence, sometimes param is prefixed to Ishvara to make it Parameshvara meaning the super controller as opposed to souls, which are mini-controllers exploiting the material energy.

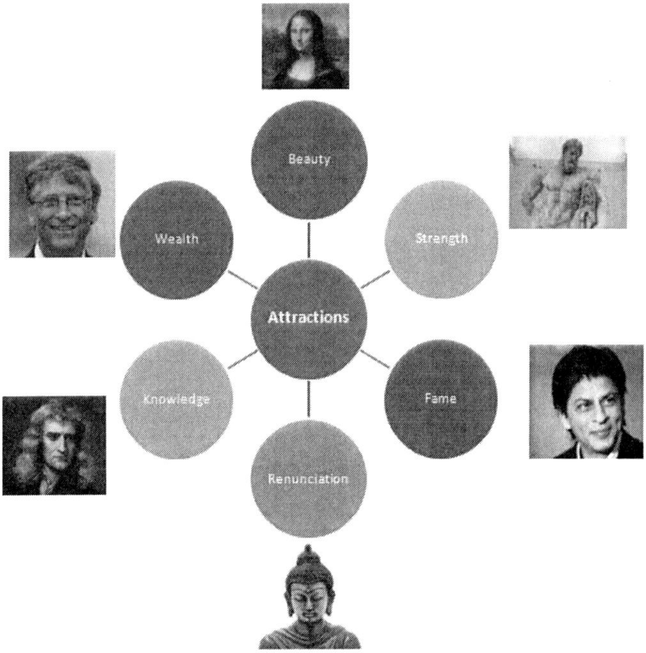

The six opulences of Bhagavan

I had already briefly mentioned to you the term Bhagavan which is how Krishna is referred to in the Bhagavad Gita. Vishnu Purana in Verse 6.5.47 describes God with the set of attributes—someone who has the six opulences of beauty, wealth, strength, knowledge, fame and renunciation in full. Adjectives have been used extensively to expound certain aspects of God. For example, Krishna means "all-attractive" and Rama means "reservoir of pleasure". The Bhagavad Gita, which is essentially a song, takes poetic liberty of describing Bhagavan in great detail when Arjuna urged Krishna to tell him about the mystic power of His opulences in full.

Krishna replied, "I will tell you of my splendorous manifestations, but only of those which are prominent, O Arjuna, for my opulences are limitless. Neither the hosts of demigods, nor the great sages know my origin, for, in every respect, I am the source of the demigods and sages. I am the source of the entire creation, and into me again it dissolves. Everything rests upon me as pearls are strung on a thread. The splendour of the Sun, which dissipates the darkness of this whole world, comes from me. And the splendour of the Moon and the splendour of fire are also from me. I enter into each planet, and by my energy they stay in orbit. I am the original fragrance of the earth, and I am the heat in fire. I am the life of all that lives, and I am the penances of all ascetics. I am the original seed of all existences, the intelligence of the intelligent, and the prowess of all-powerful men. By all the vedas am I to be known; indeed I am the compiler of vedanta, and I am the knower of the vedas. Intelligence, knowledge, freedom from doubt and delusion, forgiveness, truthfulness, control of the senses, control of the mind, happiness and distress, birth, death, fear, fearlessness, non-violence, equanimity, satisfaction, austerity, charity, fame and infamy—all these various qualities of living beings are created by me alone. I am the taste of water, the light of the Sun and the Moon, the syllable Oṁ in the vedic mantras; I am the sound in ether and ability in man. Among the 12 Adityas, (sons of Aditi and Kashyapa—Vivasvan, Aryama, Pusa, Tvasta, Savita, Bhaga, Dhata, Vidhata, Varuṇa, Mitra, Satru and Urukrama), I am Vishnu (in avatar of Urukrama or Vamana); among the luminaries, I am the radiant Sun; among the 49 Maruts, I am Marici; and among the guardians of night, I am the Moon. Among the eleven Rudras (gods of destruction), I am Shiva; and among the Yakaas and Raksasas, I am the lord of wealth (Kuvera). Among the eight Vasus, I am the god of fire (Agni); and among the mountains, I am the Meru. Of priests, O Arjuna, know me to be the chief, Brhaspati. Of generals, I am Kartikeya, and of bodies of water, I am the ocean. Of the great sages, I am Bhrgu; of vibrations, I am the transcendental Oṁ. Of sacrifices, I am the chanting of the holy names (*japa*), and of immovable things, I am the Himalayas. Of all trees, I am the banyan tree, and of the sages among the demigods, I am Narada. Of the Gandharvas, I am Citraratha, and among perfected beings, I am the sage Kapila. Of the vedas, I am the Sama Veda; of the demigods, I am Indra, the king of heaven; of the senses, I am the mind; and I am intelligence among living beings. Of horses, know me to be Uccaihsrava, produced during the churning of the ocean for nectar. Of lordly elephants, I am Airavata, and among men, I am the monarch. Of weapons, I am the thunderbolt; among cows, I am the Surabhi. Of causes for procreation, I am Kandarpa, the god of love, and of serpents, I am Vasuki. Of the many-hooded Nagas, I am Ananta, and among the aquatics, I am the demigod Varuṇa. Of departed ancestors, I am *Aryamā*, and among the dispensers of law, I am Yama, the lord of death. Of feminities, I am Kirti, Vak, Smrti, Medha, Dhrit and Ksama. Among the Daityas or demons, I am the devoted Prahlada; among subduers, I am time; among beasts, I am the lion and among birds, I am Garuda. Of purifiers, I am the wind, of the wielders of weapons, I am Rama, of fishes, I am the shark, and of flowing rivers, I am the Ganges. Of all sciences, I am the spiritual science of the self, and among logicians, I am the conclusive truth. Of letters, I am the letter A, and among compound words, I am the dual compound. I am also inexhaustible time, and of creators, I am Brahma. Of the hymns in the Sama Veda, I am the Brhat-sama, and of poetry, I am the Gayatri. Of months, I am Margasirsa (November-December), and of seasons, I am flower-bearing spring. I am gambling among deceitful practices, and the glory of the glorious. I am the victory of the victorious, the resolve of the resolute, the goodness of the good. Of the descendants of Vrsni, I am Vasudeva, and of the Pandavas, I am Arjuna. Of the sages, I am Vyasa, and among great thinkers, I am Usana. Among all means of suppressing lawlessness, I am punishment, and of those who seek victory, I am morality. Of secret things, I am silence, and of the wise, I am the wisdom. Of all creations, I am the beginning and the end and also the middle, O Arjuna. I am the all-destroying Death that annihilates all, and the origin of all that are to be born. I am the generating seed of all existences. There is no being—moving or non-moving—that can exist without Me. O mighty conqueror of enemies, there is no end to My divine manifestations. What I have spoken to you is but a mere indication of my infinite opulences. Know that all opulent, beautiful and glorious creations spring from but a spark of My splendour. But, of what avail to thee is the knowledge of all these details, O Arjuna? Suffice it to say that with a single fragment of myself I pervade and support this entire universe."

Having thus heard the glories of Bhagavan, Arjuna desired to see the Vishwarupa or Universal Form of Krishna and requested, "I have heard from you in detail about the appearance and disappearance of every living entity and have realized Your inexhaustible glories. O greatest of all personalities, O supreme form, though I see you here before me in your actual position, as you have described yourself, I wish to see how you have entered into this cosmic manifestation. I want to see that form of yours. If you think that I am able to behold your cosmic form, O my Lord, O master of all mystic power, then kindly show me that unlimited universal self."

Krishna obliged and said, "My dear Arjuna, O son of Pṛthā (Kunti), see now my opulences, hundreds of thousands of varied divine and multicoloured forms. See here the different manifestations of Adityas, Vasus, Rudras, Asvini-kumaras and all the other demigods. Behold the many wonderful things which no one has ever seen or heard of before. O Arjuna, whatever you wish to see, behold at once in this body of mine! This universal form can show you whatever you now desire to see and whatever you may want to see in the future. Everything—moving and non-moving—is here completely, in one place. But you cannot see me with your present eyes. Therefore, I give you divine eyes. Behold my mystic opulence!" Having said this Krishna took on Vishwarupa or the universal form.

Vishwarupa avatar of Krishna

In that form, Arjuna saw unlimited mouths, unlimited eyes, unlimited wonderful visions. The form was decorated with many celestial ornaments and bore many divine upraised weapons. He wore celestial garlands and garments, and many divine scents were smeared over His body. Everything was wondrous, brilliant, unlimited, all-expanding. If hundreds of thousands of suns were to rise at once into the sky, their radiance might resemble the effulgence of the Supreme Person in that universal form.

At that time Arjuna could see in the universal form of the Lord, the unlimited expansions of the universe situated in one place although divided into many, many thousands. Seeing this, bewildered and astonished Arjuna with his hair standing on an end reverently bowed his head to offer obeisances and with folded hands uttered, "My dear Lord Krishna, I see assembled in your body all the demigods and various other living entities. I see Brahma sitting on the lotus flower, as well as Lord Shiva and all the sages and divine serpents. O Lord of the universe, O universal form, I see in your body many, many arms, bellies, mouths and eyes, expanded everywhere, without limit. I see in you no end, no middle and no beginning. Your form is difficult to see because of its glaring effulgence, spreading on all sides, like blazing fire or the immeasurable radiance of the Sun. Yet I see this glowing form everywhere, adorned with various crowns, clubs and discs. You are the supreme indestructible worthy of being known; you are the ultimate refuge of this universe. You are, again, the protector of the ageless Dharma; I consider you to be the eternal imperishable being. You are without origin, middle or end. Your glory is unlimited. You have numberless arms, and the Sun and the Moon are your eyes. I see you with blazing fire coming forth from your mouth, burning this entire universe by your own radiance. Although you are one, you spread throughout the sky and the planets and all space between. O great one, seeing this wondrous and terrible form, all the planetary systems are perturbed. All the hosts of demigods are surrendering before you and entering into you. Some of them, very much afraid, are offering prayers with folded hands. Hosts of great sages and perfected beings, crying "All peace!" are praying to you by singing the Vedic hymns. All the various manifestations of Lord Shiva, the Adityas, the Vasus, the Sadhyas, the Visvedevas, the two Asvis, the Maruts, the forefathers, the Gandharvas, the Yaksas, the Asuras and the perfected demigods are beholding you in wonder. Lord, seeing this stupendous and dreadful form of yours, possessing numerous mouths and eyes, many arms, thighs and feet, many bellies and many teeth, the worlds are terror-struck; so am I. O all-pervading Visnu, seeing you with your many radiant colours touching the sky, your gaping mouths, and your great glowing eyes, my mind is perturbed by fear. I can no longer maintain my steadiness or equilibrium of mind. Lord of lords, O refuge of the worlds, please be gracious to me. I cannot keep my balance seeing thus your blazing deathlike faces and awful teeth. In all directions, I am bewildered. As the myriad streams of rivers rush towards the sea alone, so do those warriors of the mortal world enter your flaming mouths. I see all people rushing full speed into your mouths, as moths dash to destruction in a blazing fire. O Visnu, I see you devouring all people from all sides with your flaming mouths. Covering all the universe with your effulgence, you are manifest with terrible, scorching rays. O master of the senses, the world becomes joyful upon hearing your name, and thus everyone becomes attached to you. Although the perfected beings offer you their respectful homage, the demons are afraid, and they flee here and there. O great one, greater even than Brahma, you are the original creator. O limitless one, God of gods, refuge of the universe! You are the invincible source, the cause of all causes, transcendental to this material manifestation. You are the primal Deity, the most ancient person; you are the ultimate resort of this universe. You are both the knower of everything, and all that is knowable. You are the supreme refuge, above the material modes. O limitless form! This whole cosmic manifestation is pervaded by you! You are Vayu, Yama, Agni, Varuna, the Moon god, Brahma, nay, the father of Brahma himself. Hail, hail to you a thousand times; salutations, repeated salutations to you, once again. O Lord of infinite prowess, O soul of all, my obeisance to you from all sides indeed. You, who possesses infinite might, pervades all; therefore, you are all. You are the father of this complete cosmic manifestation, of the moving and the non-moving. You are its worshipable chief, the supreme spiritual master. No one is greater than you, nor can anyone be one with you. How then could there be anyone greater than you within the three worlds, O Lord of immeasurable power? After seeing this universal form, which I have never seen before, I am gladdened, but at the same time, my mind is disturbed with fear. Show me that (previous) form only, O God; have mercy, O God of gods, O Abode of the universe."

Thus, Krishna came back to his normal human form.'

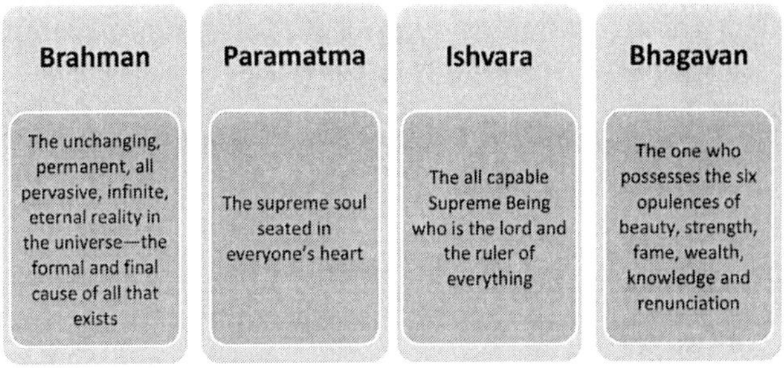

Various interpretations of the term God

'Your explanation of Brahman, Paramatma, Ishvara and Bhagavan was simply beautiful. I have also heard that we are God—*Aham Brahmāsmi*. Is that true?' I enquired further.

'That is a totally wrong understanding of the Brahma Sutra "*Aham Brahmāsmi*". *Aham Brahmāsmi* doesn't mean that you are Brahman. Rather it means that you are part of Brahman, meaning you are similar to Brahman in quality but not in quantity. By definition, Brahman, which means big, cannot be something as small as an individual person. It is a bit like a drop of water and the ocean. Both the drop and the ocean have exactly the same property but a drop is not ocean just as a spark has all the qualities of fire but is not fire. This analogy explains "*Achintya Bheda Abheda*" or the simultaneous oneness and difference between Brahman and the soul. I had explained to you earlier that God is not just the creator but also all creation. So yes, in that sense you are God but just in part. Saying that because you are a part that is why you are God would be saying that a brick is a house whereas a brick is only a part of the entire house. Also, the Paramatma concept of God explains that God is seated inside you. So, God is within you, but you are not God.'

'So who am I?' I asked.

'You are an embodied soul—a soul which is covered by material body. The Bhagavad Gita (verses 7.4 and 7.5) says, "Earth, water, fire, air, ether, mind, intelligence and false ego—together these eight constitute my separated material energies. Besides these, there is another superior energy of mine which comprises the living entities who are exploiting the resources of this material, inferior nature." So essentially you are a soul, which is the superior energy of the lord and exploits this inferior material world. You are superior because unlike the inferior material energy, you are conscious. The soul is superior not only because it is eternal, unlike the material world comprising earth, water, fire, air, ether, mind, intelligence and false ego which is ephemeral, but also because the soul can control this material world—not fully but at least to some extent. If the soul could control the material energy fully then it would be Parameshvara or Supreme Controller. So although as souls we are superior to material energy, we are still subordinate to Parameshvara.

If you look around, all life forms, from a tiny mosquito to the mighty humans, are doing nothing but exploiting the eight-fold material energy comprising earth, water, fire, air, ether, mind, intelligence and false ego. You could be a top industrialist or a humble peasant, no matter what your profession is, you are just exploiting the five gross elements or panchamahabhuta and three subtle elements of mind, intelligence and false ego.

At a more fundamental level, you are part of *prakriti* or nature as opposed to the creator who is Purusha. If purusha is the enjoyer then prakriti is all that is to be enjoyed. If purusha is the masculine, then prakriti is feminine. Prakriti again is of two types—inferior and superior. The inferior is called *apara prakriti* or the material energy and the superior is called *para prakriti* or the spiritual energy. The spiritual world is eternal while material world is constantly changing by going into cycles of creation and destruction. Our souls are spiritual while our bodies are material. It is the spiritual that exploits the material. The soul is called marginal energy as it can live in both apara prakriti or para prakriti. The true and permanent home of the soul however is in para prakriti or the spiritual world as explained in the Bhagavad Gita (Verse

8.21), "This unmanifested and the imperishable is the highest goal. Those who reach it do not return to this samsara or the cycle of birth and death. That is my supreme abode."'

'And how to reach this supreme abode?' I asked.

YOGA

'Through yoga,' Charan responded.

'You mean through exercising?' I asked unconvinced.

Charan lamented, 'It is a pity that the modern understanding of yoga is merely physical exercises. As I mentioned to you earlier yoga is not turning and twisting the body. The Sanskrit word 'yoga' means union.'

'Union with whom or with what?' I asked.

'With the Brahman. The Bhagavad Gita (Verse 14.26) says, "Those who serve me with unalloyed yoga of devotion transcend the three modes of material nature and come to the level of Brahman."'

'What are these three modes of material nature?' I wondered.

'The three modes or gunas are sattva, rajas and tamas about which I briefly mentioned to you earlier. Rajas creates future, sattva maintains the present and tamas turns the present into past. In the Bhagavad Gita (Verse 18.40), Krishna declares that "whether on the Earth or again among the demigods in the higher heaven, there exists not a single being, which is free from these three modes, born of the material-nature". Thus, the gunas grip everyone on the Earth and heavens alike. Only in vaikuntha or spiritual world, one is free from the clutches of guna. The first guna is sattva guna or the mode of goodness, which the Bhagavad Gita (Verse 14.6) defines as the one, "which is purer than the other modes, is illuminating, and which frees one from all sinful reactions. Those situated in that mode become conditioned by a sense of happiness and knowledge."

The next mode is raja guna or rajas—the mode of passion, which the Bhagavad Gita (Verse 14.7) defines as "born of unlimited desires and longings because of which the embodied living entity is bound to material fruitive actions."

And finally, there is tama guna or tamas—the mode of ignorance, which is described in the Bhagavad Gita (Verse 14.8) as "delusion of all embodied living entities. The results of this mode are negligence, indolence and sleep".

The Bhagavad Gita (verses 14.9, 14.17 and 14.18) explain further that "the mode of goodness conditions one to happiness; passion conditions one to fruitive action; and ignorance, covering one's knowledge, binds one to madness. From the mode of goodness, real knowledge develops; from the mode of passion, greed develops; and from the mode of ignorance develops foolishness, negligence and illusion. Those situated in the mode of goodness gradually go upward to the higher planets; those in the mode of passion live on the earthly planets; and those in the abominable mode of ignorance go down to the hellish worlds. Men in the mode of goodness worship the demigods or devas; those in the mode of passion worship the demons or Yaksas-raksamsi; and those in the mode of ignorance worship ghosts and spirits". People in the mode of goodness or sattva think before they act, people in the mode of passion or rajas act before they think, and people in the mode of ignorance or tamas merely wonder what has happened. All jivas are acting under the influence of these three modes. In fact, as I mentioned to you that different permutations and combinations of these three gunas produce millions of species. These gunas affect every aspect of our life.'

'What kind of aspects?' I asked.

'Everything, from food to austerity to charity. One who has a preponderance of tamas is under the influence of spiritual ignorance, is foolish, idle, senseless and given to dreaming, unenergetic, swayed by anger and haughtiness. One who is outgoing, vocal, skillful in managing others, free from envy, always active, full of hubris and of hot temperament is said to be under the influence of rajas. And one who is wise, patient, has no relish for starting new projects, free from fault-finding, and free from anger, wise and forbearing is said to be under the influence of sattva.

The Bhagavad Gita (verses 17.8 to 17.10) mentions, "Persons in the mode of goodness prefer food that promotes the lifespan and increases virtue, strength, health, happiness and satisfaction. Such kinds of food are juicy, succulent, nourishing and naturally tasteful. Food that is too bitter, too sour, salty, very hot, pungent, dry, and spicy, is dear to people in the mode of passion. Such food causes pain, grief and disease. Food that is overcooked, stale, putrid, polluted, and impure is dear to people in the mode of ignorance."

The Bhagavad Gita (verses 17.17 to 17.19) mentions, "When devout persons with ardent faith practise austerities without yearning for material rewards, they are designated as austerities in the mode of goodness. The austerity that is performed with ostentation for the sake of gaining honour, respect and adoration is in the mode of passion. Its benefits are unstable and transitory. The austerity that is performed by those with confused notions, and which involves torturing the self or harming others, is described to be in the mode of ignorance."

The Bhagavad Gita (verses 17.19 to 17.21) mentions, "Charity given out of duty, without expectation of return, at the proper time and place, and to a worthy person is considered to be in the mode of goodness. Charity given with reluctance, with the hope of a return or in expectation of a reward, is said to be in the mode of passion. And charity performed at an impure place, at an improper time, to unworthy persons, or without proper attention and respect is said to be in the mode of ignorance."

As you can see the behaviour of people depends on the guna or the mode they are influenced by. In fact, the gunas are so powerful that they effect what body you will get in your next birth. The Bhagavad Gita (Verse 13.22) says, "*kaaranam guna-sango sya sad-asad-yoni-janmasu*", meaning that soul gets the body of higher or lower species of life depending on its association with the gunas or modes of nature. Depending on which guna the soul associates with, a matching body is granted in the next life.'

'I am a bit lost here. Earlier, you had mentioned that the laws of karma affect the journey of souls including the type of body they get in their next life. But now you are saying that the gunas of the material nature control that. So, which one is it?' I was utterly confused.

'Very good question! You are right—the laws of karma control everything. Let's look at it from the beginning. What happens when you smoke a cigarette for the first time?'

'Well, I did try once in my university and I started coughing violently.'

'Did you try again?'

'Hmm...actually I did. We were having a late-night party, and someone offered me. I could not refuse.'

'How was the experience the second time?'

'Well, it was a lot easier to try the second time. The first time I was a bit hesitant, but the second time it was easier and I did not cough as badly as the first time.'

'Was that the last time?'

'To be honest, no,' I said a bit embarrassed.

Charan soothed me, 'I am not trying to make you uneasy. I am just trying to explain to you how we have a greater propensity to do something that we have done once. The second time we are slightly less hesitant and before long it becomes a habit. This, by the way, works not just for cigarettes but for everything. The first time you write an exam it appears hard and then it gets easier. The first time you do charity, it is difficult to part with your hard-earned money but then it becomes easier. This is the binding property of the gunas—the propensity to do more of the same that we have done before.

Imagine that there are two dogs inside you—one good and one bad. Both of them are equally powerful. The first time you feed either of these, it gets slightly more powerful than the other. The next time that slightly more powerful dog is better equipped to snatch the food off your hands compared to the other dog. Eventually, the time will come that one of the dogs is super big and powerful while the other one is meek and almost dying so that you can't even feel it exists.

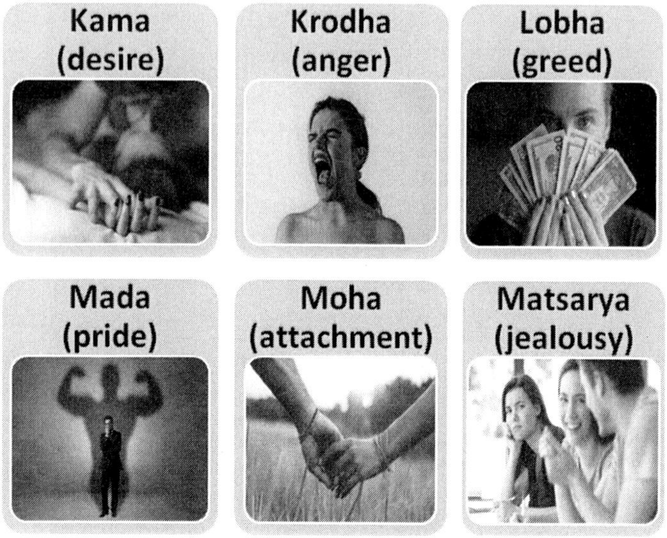

Shadripu or the six vices

The choice of which dog we want to feed is totally ours—good or bad. The bad dog is *shadripu* (the six enemies) and the good dog is *shadguna* (the six virtues). Shadripu are mentioned in Devi Bhagavad Purana (Verse 7.35.3) as kama (desire), *krodha* (anger), *lobha* (greed), *mada* (pride), *moha* (attachment) and *matsarya* (jealousy):

kāmakrōdhau lōbhamōhau madamātsaryasañjñakau

The great Indian philosopher Adi Shankaracharya says, *"Kama Krodascha Lobhascha Dehe Thishtanthi Taskarah Jnana Ratno-paharaya Tasmat Jagrata Jagrata"*, meaning beware of the enemies of desire, anger and greed making a comfortable residence lying in an ambush of the heart awaiting to steal away the precious gem of wisdom or *gyana*.

The Bhagavad Gita (Verse 16.21)—*'tri-vidhaṁ narakasyedaṁ dvāraṁ nāśanam ātmanaḥ kāmaḥ krodhas tathā lobhas'*—illustrates the same point: "There are three gates leading to hell—desire, anger and greed." Our greatest enemies are not outside but within us! In modern times, we are continuously bombarded with objects of sense gratification—newer models of phones, ever-changing fashion, latest movies, catchy music, exotic holiday locations and many more. We are inundated with advertisements shown on the Internet, television, magazines and newspapers. We see our friends and relatives boast about such objects on social media. It is hard to resist the temptation. We tend to focus only on the nice things, which others are apparently enjoying and become totally oblivious to their sufferings and compromises.

We tend to equate happiness with money, power and prestige. We get attracted, develop an attachment to these sense objects and soon they become a must-have for us and on our wish list. We fall into the illusion that unless we get a particular object or position, we cannot be happy. As a result, we are always chasing sense gratification and seeking a sense of pleasure. Such attachment is called moha and the persistent chasing is a resultant of lobha.

From moha or attachment comes a strong desire or kama to enjoy these objects of sense gratification. This desire intensifies into lobha or greed. In the Bhagavad Gita (verses 2.62 and 2.63), Krishna explains to Arjuna about anger and desire, "from attachments, desire is born; from desire, anger rises; from anger comes delusion; from delusion comes the loss of memory; from loss of memory comes the destruction of discrimination; from the destruction of discrimination one perishes".

Once we get the object of our pursuit and achieve slightly more than others, we become drunk with mada or pride. Pride is the feeling of self-worth derived from the pleasure one gets in one's own achievement of wealth, fame, prestige or power. This pride is our enemy because it becomes a hurdle in maintaining a cordial relationship with others.

On the other hand, if we don't achieve what we desire while others do, we develop a feeling of matsarya or jealousy towards them. Jealousy results from a strong lust to possess something achieved by others. The moment we see our colleagues or our neighbours, or our friends, or our relatives possess something that we yearn for, we become envious.

Shadgunas or the six virtues

Contrasting the shadripu are the *shadgunas* or the six virtues. They are described by sage Valmiki in Chapter 33 of the 'Ayodhya Kanda' of the great epic Ramayana:

> ānṛśaṁsyam anukrośaḥ śrutaṁ śīlaṁ damaḥ śamaḥ
> rāghavaṁ śobhayanti ete ṣaḍ guṇāḥ puruṣottamaṁ
>
> —Ramayana (Verse 2.33.12)

It means non-violence (*anrisham*), compassion (*anukrosham*), learning (*shrutam*), humility (*shilam*), self-control (*dama*) and equanimity (*shama*) are the six qualities that adorn Rama, the greatest among men.

The ancient Indian principle of anrisham or harmlessness (also known as *ahimsa*) towards all living beings is a key virtue inspired by the premise that all living beings have the same spark of the divine spiritual energy; therefore, to hurt another being is to hurt oneself. Any violence has karmic consequences. Anrisham's precept of 'cause no injury' includes not only one's deeds but also words and thoughts. Willful harm to other life forms must be avoided. Wars must be shunned, with sincere and truthful dialogue as far as possible. One of the most popular advocates of the principle of anrisham in recent times was Mahatma Gandhi.

The virtue of anukrosham (also known as *karuna*) refers to compassion or empathy upon seeing another person's suffering. The essence of it is codified in the Ramayana, Verse 2.2.40 of Chapter 2 of 'Ayodhya Kanda': *'vyasanēṣu manuṣyāṇāṅ bhṛśaṅ bhavati duḥkhitaḥ utsavēṣu ca sarvēṣu pitēva parituṣyati.* It means "one who grieves profoundly when he sees someone else's suffering and rejoices upon seeing someone else's joy".

The virtue of shrutam means hearing or listening. More specifically it means learning by listening. Historically, in India knowledge was transferred from one generation to the next by students hearing from their teachers. The vedas are considered the primary source of knowledge and are, in fact, synonymous with the term *shruti,* which means 'to hear'. Students chant the vedas verbatim as they learn from their teachers and thus preserve the knowledge of the vedas orally. The vedas have been transferred like this from one generation to the next for thousands of years. Vedic chanting has been inscribed by UNESCO as Intangible Cultural Heritage of Humanity.[28] All the *shad darshanas* or six orthodox schools of Indian philosophy accept the authority of shruti, i.e., the vedas. Manu Smriti (Chapter 2, Verse 10) states *srutistu vedo vigneya,* which means, "know that Vedas are shruti". Chapter 2, Verse 13 further says, "Dharma jijñāsamānam pramāṇam paramam śrutih" meaning "to those who seek the knowledge of dharma, the supreme authority is shruti".

The virtue of shilam refers to good conduct or humility. The motto of Lal Bahadur Shastri National Academy of Administration in India which trains civil servants such as IAS, IFS, and IPS, the country's top most bureaucrats, is the famous quote from *Niti Shatakam* written by Bhartrahari, which says "*sheelam param bhushanam*" meaning "humility or good conduct is the supreme ornament".

The virtues of dama and shama are in pairs. Dama refers to control of sense and shama is all about steadiness of mind or equanimity. The Katha Upanishad mentions the senses which are like the vicious wild horses pulling the mind in all directions. When the mind is overpowered by any one of these senses running wild, one loses the ability to reason and becomes like a ship tossed by storms upon the high ocean. Dama and shama both have been defined as virtues at multiple places in the Bhagavad Gita and Shrimad Bhagavatam.

If you think of it carefully, the good dog or shadguna is diametrically opposite of the bad dog or shadripu. Anrisham is the antidote to krodha, anukrosham removes matsarya, shrutam counters moha, shilam diminishes mada, dama conquers kama and shama kills lobha.

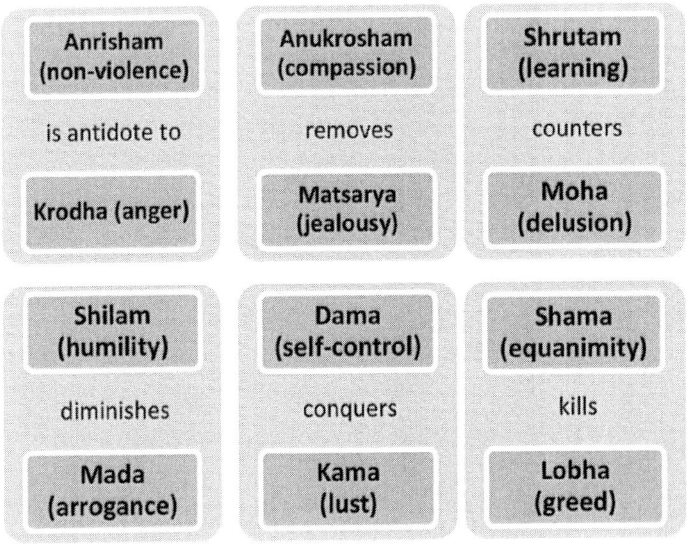

Shadguna annihilates Shadripu

The law of karma gives you the free will to feed whichever dog you want—good dog or bad dog. But once you feed either of these dogs, do remember that one of them will become more powerful than the other. So yes, your karma controls everything but what kriya you are likely to do is controlled by the gunas. You have free will and you must use it judiciously to decide which of the three—goodness, passion or ignorance—you want to feed and be influenced by. If you imagine yourself as a puppet, then the three modes of goodness, passion and ignorance are the strings attached to you. Whichever mode you feed, will get more power to pull you in its direction the next time and your karma will get updated accordingly.'

'You have explained it beautifully. I understood that the mode acting on us will influence our karma accordingly. But it seems like no matter what choice you make, you will keep accruing karma pulled by either ignorance, passion or goodness. But you mentioned that the goal of life is akarma. How can we strive for akarma when these modes are so powerful and pulling you all the time?'

'You are absolutely right Anveshak. The gunas are very powerful and it is not easy to escape their influence. But before we learn about transcending the modes of the material nature, let's first look at the behaviour of someone who has transcended the three modes.

In the Bhagavad Gita (verses 14.22 to 14.25), Krishna tells Arjuna, "He who does not hate illumination, attachment and delusion when they are present or long for them when they disappear; who is unwavering and undisturbed through all these reactions of the material qualities, remaining neutral and transcendental, knowing that the modes alone are active; who is situated in the self and regards alike happiness and distress; who looks upon a lump of earth, a stone and a piece of gold with an equal eye; who is equal towards the desirable and the undesirable; who is steady, situated equally well in praise and blame, honour and dishonour; who treats alike both friend and enemy; and who has renounced all material activities—such a person is said to have transcended the modes of nature."'

I reasoned, 'Even the description of this makes me feel that this is an extremely hard stage to reach. Sounds like the very definition of stoicism.'

'That is why we have yoga to help us reach there.' Charan said.

'Yoga?' I asked puzzled.

He elaborated, 'The purpose of yoga is to connect with the Brahman. One who is connected to Brahman is detached from this material world. The three modes only operate in the material world. The more advanced one gets in one's *yoga saadhana* or yoga practice, the closer one gets to the Brahman and the less affected one is by the modes of the material nature. In *ayoga* or disconnect with the material world lies the yoga or union with the Brahman. In the Bhagavad Gita (Verse 6.46), Krishna tells Arjuna, "A yogi is higher than men of austerity; he is considered higher than men of knowledge. The yogi is also higher than men of fruitive action. Therefore, O Arjuna, be a yogi."'

'And who is a yogi?' I quizzed.

'One who is merely performing physical exercises for good health is not a yogi. Neither is the one having extraordinary magical powers or even the one who has matted locks of hair sitting in austere meditation in the Himalayas. A yogi is one who is following one of the four bonafide yogas.'

'What are these four bona fide yogas?' I was dazed.

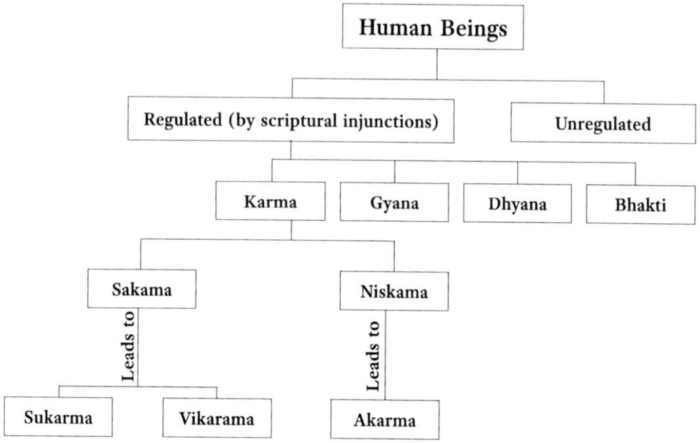

Various types of yogas

Charan began to explain, 'These are *karma yoga, gyana yoga, dhyana yoga* and *bhakti yoga.* As I have mentioned to you previously, soul is an alien in the material world. Its dharma (i.e., the holding position) is when it is in yoga or connection with the Supreme Soul—this is the intrinsic nature of the soul (to connect to the Supreme Soul). In this state, the soul realizes its innate nature of satchitananda (eternal, superconscious and blissful). Yoga is the process of establishing this connection. There are millions and millions of humans who are totally oblivious to the four paths of yoga and lead their lives in unregulated ways. These unregulated people do not believe in soul, rebirth or karma. Such people are called *nastika.*'

I interjected, 'Nastika as in atheist?'

Charan replied, 'Not exactly. Although the word 'nastika' and 'atheist' are used interchangeably, they do not mean the same thing. This is again a mistranslation. Let's break down the two words. The etymological root for the word 'atheism' originated before the fifth century BC from the ancient Greek word '*ἄθεος*' (atheos), meaning "without god(s)". So, an atheist is one who "does not believe in the existence of theos or gods". On the other hand, the Sanskrit word '*asti*' etymologically means "there is". So *astika* refers to someone who "believes there is" while nastika is someone who "believes there isn't". But what do we mean by "there is" or "there isn't"? To understand this, we need to visit the great Sanskrit grammarian Panini. If you see carefully, unlike the word 'atheist', the word 'nastika' does not categorically spell out "there is no God".

In *Ashtadhyayi* Verse 4.4.60—'*Asti-nāsti-diṣṭam.matiḥ*'—Panini explains the meaning of the terms astika and nastika. Kasika, the foremost commentator on *Ashtadhyayi*, explains the sutra as "*paralokosti iti yasy matih sa aastikah tadvipareeto naastikah*", meaning anyone who believes in a hereafter or other world, i.e., *paraloka*, is an astika and who does not is a nastika. Hence, as you can see, atheist is one who believes there is no God while nastika is one who believes there is no afterworld.'

I commented, 'Great etymological derivation but what difference does it make in the practical world? Aren't both the words 'nastika' and 'atheist' implying the same thing?'

Charan elaborated, 'Absolutely not! There is a big difference. Indian philosophy has various schools such as Nyaya, Vaisheshika, Sankhya, Patanjali Yoga, Mimamsa, Vedanta, Buddhism, Jainism and Ajivika. The word 'darshana' literally means to see. The pragmatic meaning of darshana is vision of life, i.e., the philosophy of life. The first six darshanas are collectively called shad darshana (the six philosophies), while the latter three are collectively called *shramana darshana* (philosophy of those who toil—implying the seekers who perform acts of austerity). From a theistic point of view, i.e., believing in God, the shad darshana of Nyaya, Vaisheshika, Sankhya, Patanjali Yoga, Mimamsa and Vedanta are theistic schools while the shramana darshana of Jainism, Buddhism and Ajivika are atheistic schools.'

I was stunned and protested, 'How can Buddhism and Jainism be atheistic schools?'

Charan responded, 'Because they are! They are atheists but not nastika.'

With a baffled look I said, 'Atheists but not nastika?'

Charan explained, 'There is no concept of creator or God in Jainism or Buddhism. They are non-theistic religions. Contrary to the popular belief, both Jain Tirthankara Mahavira and Gautama Buddha are regarded as spiritual teachers and not gods in Jainism and Buddhism, respectively. However, the concepts of soul, karma and afterlife do exist in Jainism. Buddhists believe in consciousness after death, karma and rebirth. Ajivikas or Fatalists do not believe in Creator God. However, they believe that in every living being there is a soul that passes through many births and ultimately progresses unto its pre-destined *nirvana* (salvation). The Ajivika school is known for its *niyati* (or destiny) doctrine of absolute determinism—everything is predetermined. The premise is that there is no free will. Everything that has happened, is happening and will happen is entirely preordained and a function of cosmic principles. Ajivikas consider the doctrine of karma a fallacy. On the other hand, both Buddhists and Jains believe in the doctrine of karma with a nuanced difference. Buddhists believe that only wilful actions have consequences, ignorance or actions done without intent do not have consequences. Jains believe that all actions have consequences whether intentional or unintentional. Jain monks cover their mouths and carry a broom to clear their way so as not to even accidentally harm any living being that they may ingest or tread upon.

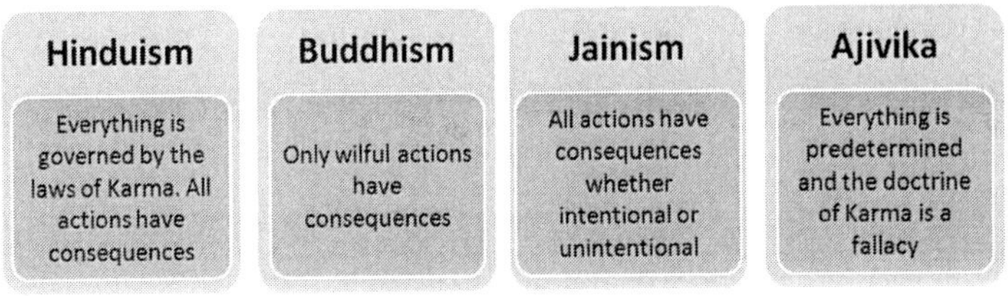

Karma in different schools of Indian philosophy

All the three shramana schools of Jainism, Buddhism and Ajivika do not presume any deity as the creator of the universe. And hence are atheistic. One interesting fact is that Chandragupta Maurya, the founder of the Mauryan Empire, in 322 BC, embraced Jainism while his son Bindusara followed Ajivika and his grandson Ashoka adopted Buddhism. Ashoka sponsored Buddhist missionaries in Sri Lanka, Central Asia, Southeast Asia, Egypt and Hellenistic Europe, which greatly expanded the spread of Indian philosophies outside India.

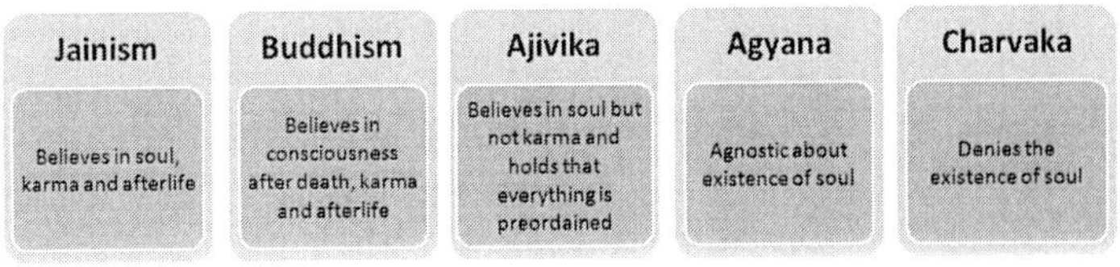

Atheistic schools of Indian philosophy

Beyond the six shad darshanas and the three shramana schools are Agyana and Charvaka schools. The agnostic school of Agyana is known for its skepticism. They believe that it is impossible to obtain knowledge of metaphysical nature or ascertain the truth value of philosophical propositions; and even if knowledge was possible, it was useless and disadvantageous for final salvation. Their skepticism has been summed up by the ninth century Jain writer Silanka as: "Who knows that the soul exists? Of what use is this knowledge? Who knows that the soul does not exist? Of what use is this knowledge?" In contrast, the Charvaka philosophy rejects atma altogether. The Charvaka philosophy holds perception and direct experiments to be the only valid and reliable source of knowledge. This is the materialistic view, which totally disregards the spiritual existence. As per this school of philosophy, consciousness is treated as a byproduct of neuro-chemical reactions inside the brain and not the outcome of an atma inside the body.

The shad darshanas are also sometimes called orthodox Indian philosophies while the rest are sometimes referred to as the heterodox Indian philosophies. I hope you can now see how three shramana darshanas of Jainism, Buddhism and Ajivika are atheist but not nastika. Agyana is agnostic. And only Charvaka is nastika.'

I replied, 'I fully understand the difference between nastika and atheist now. You also mentioned shad darshanas. Please tell me more about them.'

Charan continued, 'Shad darshanas are the six systems of philosophies based on the Vedas. They hold Vedas as the supreme and ultimate source of knowledge unlike the shramana darshanas, which reject the authority of the Vedas.

By and large, all the six shad darshanas deal with four topics—nature of Brahman, nature of atma, creation of *jagat* or world and moksha.

The Nyaya philosophy was propounded by Akshapad Gautama in the fourth century. Nyaya meaning justice uses logical methods to establish that a collection of general or universal rules apply equally and in a just manner to all living beings without any discrimination. It states that human sufferings result from mistakes or defects produced by activities under wrong knowledge such as wrong notions or ignorance and moksha is gained through right knowledge.

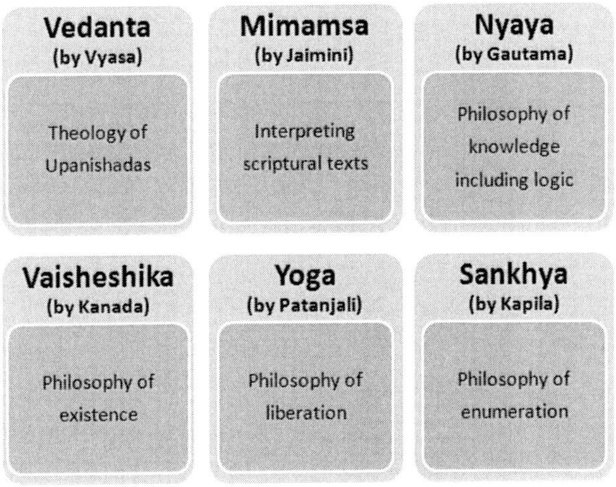

Theistic schools of Indian philosophy

Vaisheshika founded by Kanada Kashyapa around the second century BC postulates that all objects in the physical universe are composed of *paramanu* (atoms), and one's experiences are derived from the interplay of substances (a function of atoms, their count and spatial arrangements), quality, activity, commonness, particularity and inherence. Liberation is attained through understanding the nature of existence. Nyaya and Vaisheshika are viewed as a complementary pair—with Nyaya emphasizing logic and Vaisheshika analysing the nature of the world.

The literal meaning of Mimamsa is inquiry. Mimamsa was founded by Jaimini in second century BC. It teaches the correct performance of Vedic mantras and rituals ('Karma Kanda': *Samhitas* and *Brahmanas* sections of the Vedas) as the means to liberation.

On the other hand, Vedanta deals with 'Gyana Kanda' of the Vedas (*Aranyakas* and *Upanishads*) focusing on meditation, reflection and knowledge of Self, Oneness, and Brahman. There are various commentaries on the Vedanta. The best known among them are Advait or non-dualistic commentaries by Shankara, Dvaita or dualistic form by Madhava, Vishishtadvaita or qualified non-dualistic commentaries by Ramanuja, Dvaitavaita commentaries by Nimbarka and Shudhadvait commentaries by Vallabha. Mimamsa and Vedanta are considered to be a pair. In fact, they are sometimes called Purva Mimamsa or Early Mimamsa, dealing with the earlier portions of the Vedas, and Uttara Mimamsa or Late Mimamsa, dealing with the later portion of the Vedas (i.e., the Vedantas).

Sankhya Philosophy or literally the philosophy of numeration or the one relating to numbers was propounded by the sage Kapila in the fifth century BC. The philosophy revolves around the interaction of prakriti and purusha. Moving on, Patanjali Yoga is a philosophy and practice codified by Patanjali in *Yoga Sutras* in second century BC. Its objective is to achieve, at will, the cessation of all fluctuations of consciousness, and the attainment of self-realization. Sankhya and Yoga are considered an inseparable pair.'

'Thank you so much for the detailed explanation of the six darshanas. You were talking about unregulated and regulated people when we went deep into the discussion of astika and nastika. You mentioned that unregulated people do not believe in soul, rebirth or karma. What are the regulated ones doing?' I asked.

Charan explained, 'The regulated people try to follow one of the four bona fide yoga paths of *karma yoga, gyana yoga, dhyana yoga* or *bhakti yoga* in their quest to reconnect with the Supreme. The karma yogi vehemently believes in the Bhagavad Gita (Verse 2.47):

karmany evadhikaras te ma phalesu kadacana
ma karma-phala-hetur bhur ma te sango 'stv akarmani

It means, "You have a right to perform your prescribed duty, but you are not entitled to the fruits of action. Never consider yourself to be the cause of the results of your activities, and never be attached to not doing your duty." Such a yogi is following nishkama karma or executing his duties without any expectations in return and is a true karma yogi. One who has given up attachment to the reward of actions and who is free from the ego sense of 'I', 'my', and 'mine' has no connection to reactions arising from any action.

The Bhagavad Gita (Verse 18.14) describes five factors—the physical platform (body), ego, organs, effort and divine—as responsible for reactions from any action. We can only tame the ego. It is impossible to eliminate the other four factors. Can you remove your body or organs, or effort, or the divine will from any action? The only thing you can eliminate is your egoistic sense of being the doer. One needs to understand that one is not the doer but just nimittamatra or merely an instrument. One who has disassociated oneself from the egoistic perception of being the doer of action has no bearing to the karmic reactions arising from the action.

The first stage of nishkama karma yoga is sacrificing fruits of labour for charitable causes and cultivating the practice of parting with one's fruits of labour. Gradually one's mind is purified, and one begins to work without selfish desires for personal gains. When one is totally detached from the fruits of one's actions, such actions are unalloyed with desires and hence do not trigger karmic reactions. One who has perfected this art of detachment is a true karma yogi.

On the other hand, *sakama karmis* are fruitive workers, who are eager to enjoy the fruits of their labour. They are not karma yogis but *karma kandis*. They regulate their sense enjoyment, i.e., do not act whimsically, accept authorities of scriptures and vedas. Vedas are typically divided into four parts: *Samhitas*, *Brahmanas*, *Aranyakas* and *Upanishads*. *Samhitas*, which are ritualistic mantras, and *Brahmanas*, which are ritualistic explanation of the mantras, are collectively called karma-kandas. The karma kandas prescribe various rituals for the fulfilment of material desires through the worship of devas or demigods. Such individuals will gradually make progress in understanding the real purpose of life over a long period of time (maybe many lives). In another Gita, or song of Mahabharata called Vyadha Gita, the concept of karma yogi is beautifully explained.'

'What! There are more Gitas than one?' I couldn't believe what I had heard.

'Yes, there are several! Although *Gita* is generally understood to be the Bhagavad Gita, the literal meaning of the word 'gita' is song and the Bhagavad Gita, or the song of God, is not the only song or gita in the Mahabharata. Among other gitas or songs, the Mahabharata includes Pingala Gita, Vyadha Gita, Ashtavakra Gita, Anu Gita, Baka Gita, Nahusha Gita, Shaunaka Gita, Yudhishthira Gita, Parashara Gita, Bodhya Gita, Vichakshyu Gita, Manki Gita, Vritra Gita, Sampaka Gita, Harita Gita, Bhishma Gita, Brahmana Gita, Sanatsujata Gita and Vidura Gita.

Beyond the Mahabharata, there are several gitas or songs in other scriptures such as Bhikshu Gita or monk's song from Shrimad Bhagavatam, which is a brief dialogue on the exposition of the vedanta philosophy, Brahman and the atma between King Parikshit, the grandson of Arjuna, and Sage Suka; Devi Gita or the song of goddess from Devi Bhagavatam, wherein Devi describes her own nature, nature of her worship with meditation, yogic practices, rituals and other austerities; Guru Gita from Skanda Purana is a conversation between Lord Shiva and Goddess Parvati about the need for and the importance of seeking a spiritual teacher or a guru; Gopika Gita, or the song of cowherd girls from Shrimad Bhagavatam, describes the deep and selfless love of cowherd girls for Krishna; and Uddhava Gita from Shrimad Bhagvatam is Krishna's final discourse to Uddhava before Krishna leaves his mortal coil on Earth.

Among the Gitas of the Mahabharata, the Pingala Gita and Vyadha Gita are particularly interesting in the sense that they provide wisdom coming from the most unexpected people—a prostitute and a butcher.

Pingala Gita is the song of a prostitute named Pingala.

It appears in the 'Moksha Parva' as part of 'Shanti Parva' section of the Mahabharata and is the song of liberation of the prostitute Pingala. One day starting her typical daily or more precisely nightly routine, Pingala dresses and decorates herself seductively as the evening sets in to attract one of the many men who are going along the road. Evening turns to night and night to midnight, yet no one approaches her which leaves Pingala peeved. As her hopes of earning that night dry out, the perplexed, disappointed and exhausted Pingala gets into a deep self-reflection. Observing herself from an impartial perspective, she laments how she was seeking eternal happiness in the love she purchased by selling her body to customers, who were themselves tormented by lust and greed, which only brought her unhappiness, fear, anxiety, lamentation and illusion.

After discerning the worthlessness of her lovers, she then analyses the worthlessness of the other component in her pursuit of pleasure—her own body—which she realizes to be a mere complex of bones, nerves, blood vessels, skin and hair and is a nine-gated city (eyes, ears, nostrils, mouth, anus and genitals) filled with impurities. Coming to a sudden self-awareness, Pingala laments her folly in seeking worthless lovers to please her mortal body. She realizes that the world is caught in the grip of the serpent of time and when one learns to spurn desires and remains in *vairagya* or detached from these desires one is sure to gain peace of mind. She reflects on that which had earlier seemed to be a misfortune—the absence of any customer to fulfil her desire—and realizes that more desires bring more pain; no desires means no entanglements and only eternal happiness. She understands that desire is the cause of misery; freedom from desires is the cause of happiness. This great sense of detachment from desire (*asha*) awakes her and not only removes her anxiety, but also replaces it with happiness following which she peacefully sits down on her bed and happily goes to a sound sleep. Pingala realized the art of vairagya or being nishkama, i.e., detached from desires.'

Completely captivated by the fascinating narration of Pingala's detachment, I reflected, 'What a beautiful story of getting wisdom from the most unexpected person—a prostitute, who represents the archetype of lust and vices, coming to a self-realization of the futility of desires and finding solace in giving up all desires.'

Charan said, 'While Pingala Gita is the quintessence of what nishkama or desireless means, Vyadha Gita or butcher's song shows what a prime example of who a true karma yogi is. Just like Pingala was in a profession despised by many, the occupation of Vyadha or butcher is also detested by many and yet the butcher in the Vyadha Gita has more wisdom than the monk in the song.

Vyadha Gita occurs in the 'Vana Parva' section of the Mahabharata and is told to Yudhishthira, the eldest of the Pandava brothers, by the sage Markandeya. The song has three characters—a sannyasi (monk), a housewife and a vyadha. The sannyasi having left his old parents uninformed retired to a forest where he meditated and practised spiritual austerities for a long time. Once while he was seated under a tree, dry leaves fell on his head due to a fight between a crow and a crane. The angry sannyasi had developed yogic powers and burnt the birds with his mere look. This incident filled the sannyasi with arrogance.

Shortly thereafter, he headed to get *bhiksha* (alms). He

came across a house where a housewife, who was serving her ailing husband, asked him to wait. Drunk with his powers, the sannyasi thought to himself, "You wretched woman, how dare you make me wait! You do not know my powers yet" to which the housewife replied, "I am neither a crow nor a crane to be burnt." The startled sannyasi was amazed at how the ordinary housewife could read the thoughts in his mind. The housewife told him, "I did not practice any austerities but by doing my duty with cheerfulness and wholeheartedness, I have become illumined and could read your thoughts. Go to the *dharma-vyadha* (the righteous butcher) in the town of Mithila, he shall answer all your questions on dharma.'

The embarrassed sannyasi overcoming his initial hesitation heads to Mithila to see the vyadha. Upon reaching there, he questions the vyadha how he can be illuminated if he is involved in "filthy and ugly work". The wise vyadha replies, "No duty is ugly, no duty is impure. Even though the vocation one pursues may lack virtue, yet the practitioner may be unimpeachable. So, even a butcher who slaughters animals for a living may be an exemplary person. In this material world, no one experiences the consequences of someone else's karma. Whatever a person does has consequences, which that person alone experiences. And knowing this occupation of butcher to be my swadharma due to the consequences of my previous karma, I will never leave this job. As regards myself, I never intentionally harm any living being, but I do sell pork and buffalo meat. I sell meat of animals that have been slaughtered by others.

Agriculture is considered to be a praiseworthy occupation, but it is well-known that even there, great harm is done to animal life. In the operation of digging the earth and ploughing, countless creatures lurking in the ground and various other forms of animal life are destroyed. What do you think of that? O good Brahmin, rice, wheat and all other seeds that are consumed are all living organisms. What is your opinion on this matter? This whole creation, O Brahmin, is full of life, sustaining itself with food derived from other living things. Have you not noticed that fish prey upon other smaller fish? Various species of animals prey upon other species, and there are species, the members of which prey upon each other. What's your opinion on this? The injunction that people should not do harm to any creature (ahimsa) was ordained by old men, who were ignorant of biological facts, for there is no one on the face of this earth, who is free from doing injury to creatures.

After full consideration, the conclusion is irresistible that there is not a single person who is free from the sin of harming animal life. There is much that can be said of the positivity or negativity of our actions. But whoever is dedicated wholeheartedly to his own proper occupation surely acquires a good reputation. One should avoid falsehood in speech and should do good without being urged to. One should never abandon dharma due to lust, anger, or malice. O best of Brahmins, greed is said to be the repository of all sins; the greedy person who has not listened to the sound teachings of the scriptures will engage in malfeasance to satisfy his greed. On obtaining an object of desire one should not be elated, nor grieve immoderately at a loss. One should never feel depressed when financially challenged and never abandon the path of dharma. One whose actions are performed without the object of securing any personal reward, who has sacrificed all into the fire of renunciation, is a real sannyasi and is really wise.

By renouncing the objects of both pleasure and pain and by abandoning emotional attachment to material things, one may attain Brahman (Supreme Being or Liberation). Therefore, one should decrease one's attachment to the physical world. This non-attachment (ayoga) is called unification (yoga).'

The vyadha introduces the sannyasi to his parents and tells him, 'O good Brahmin, you have done wrong to your parents by leaving home without their permission to study the vedas. You have not acted properly in this matter, for your ascetic and aged parents have become entirely blind from grief in your absence. Please return home to console them. May you never abandon this supreme duty.' The sannyasi now understood his fault and why the housewife had sent him to the butcher. He understood that the housewife was merely performing her duty by attending to her ailing husband while he, in his selfish pursuit of studying the vedas, has neglected his prime duty as a son.

Having heard the unparalleled description of nishkama karma as a road to liberation, the sannyasi understood vyadha to be a true karma yogi and uttering, "It is extremely rare to discover, in our midst, a person who can so well expound the mysteries of dharma; there is scarcely one among thousands, who is so well versed in the science of dharma" takes leave of the butcher and returns to his home to diligently serve his old parents who were both blind by then.

So Anveshak, do remember that the road to liberation is nishakama karma yoga and in non-attachment to desires lies the unification with the Brahman.'

Totally absorbed in the story of the butcher, I recalled our discussion and said, 'I am mesmerized by such profound explanation of who a karma yogi is. You had also mentioned about *gyana yogi*, *dhyana yogi* and *bhakti yogi*. What do these yogis do?'

Charan explained further, 'Gyana yogis are in the process of finding the Absolute Truth (which is beyond the material world) through cultivation of philosophical knowledge. A gyana yogi understands the Absolute Truth as the Brahman—the eternal spiritual reality beyond the temporary material world. Aranyakas which are esoteric explanations of mantras and Upanishadas which are philosophical explanations of the Brahman are collectively called Gyana Kandas. Gyana Kandas are of interest to a gyana yogi. The third type of yogi is dhyana yogi.

A dhyana yogi is engaged in a meditative process to control the mind and senses and to ultimately focus one's concentration on the Supreme. Dhyana yoga has eight limbs and hence is also called *ashtanga yoga*. These are *yama* (external discipline), *niyama* (internal discipline), *asana* (yoga postures), *pranayama* (breath control), *pratyahara* (withdrawal of the senses), *dharana* (concentration), *dhyana* (meditation) and finally *samadhi* (Union).

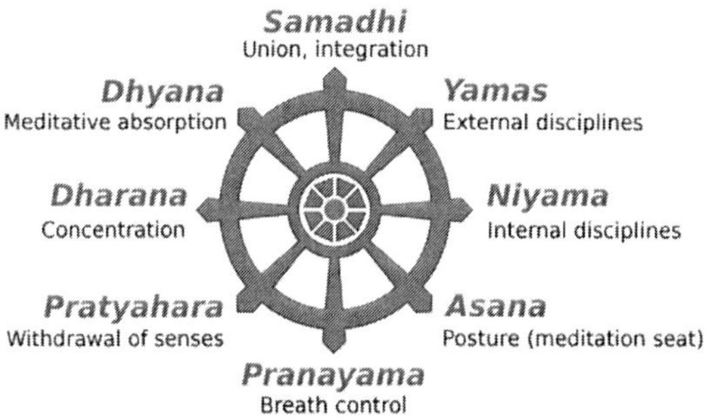

The eight limbs of Dhyana yoga.

In the initial stages, dhyana yoga involves following a strict code of conducts, practising physical and breathing exercises and meditation on the Paramatma in the heart. The final step of this yoga is actually samadhi or absorption of the self into the Brahman. Often the strict practice awards dhyana yogis with certain extraordinary powers called siddhis, which are material by-products of the dhyana yoga process. Dhyana yoga is the image people have in mind when they think of yoga—turning and twisting the body in different asanas. But as you can see different asanas are just the third ladder of dhyana yoga.

In this day and age, one can hardly reach the fourth ladder, which is of pranayama. Most people will struggle even with the first two—yama and niyama, which is essentially following what is allowed and abstaining from what is not recommended. A large number of people who claim to be doing yoga (or more accurately dhyana yoga) probably do not do it for its ultimate goal of samadhi. They are merely pursuing yoga as physical exercise. The various asanas of yoga will give them good health, but such individuals are not dhyana yogis as they are not pursuing the ultimate purpose of dhyana yoga—samadhi. The purpose of dhyana yoga is to attain a still body, still breath and still mind so that one can finally reach samadhi or oneness with the object of meditation.

It is impossible to concentrate with the mind without training the body first. The eight limbs of yoga teach us how to gradually train the body and the mind to be able to meditate on the Brahman and ultimately merge with it.

Finally, there is a bhakti yogi or devotional yogi who pursues selfless, ecstatic love of God by rendering devotional service through engaging all of one's senses in the service of the Supreme Lord who is the master of the senses. Bhakti yoga makes one transcend all material designations, purifies the heart and arouses love of God within. Shrimad Bhagavatam describes nine *margas* or paths of Bhakti Yoga—*sravanam* (hearing), *kirtanam* (speaking/singing), *smaranam* (remembering), *archanam* (worshipping the deity), *vandanam* (offering prayers), *pada sevanam* (serving the Lord's feet), *dasyam* (serving the Lord), *sakhyam* (being friends with the Lord) and *atma-nivedanam* (fully surrendering to the Lord).

Process	Meaning	Vedic character epitomizing the process
Sravanam	Hearing	Pariksit Maharaj
Kirtanam	Speaking/Singing	Sukadeva Goswami
Smaranam	Remembering	Prahlada
Arcanam	Worshiping the Deity	Prthu Maharaj
Vandanam	Offering prayers	Akrura
Pada sevanam	Serving Lord's feet	Lakshmi Devi
Dasyam	Servant	Hanuman
Sakhyam	Being friends with the Lord	Arjuna
Atma-nivedanam	Surrendering everything	Bali Maharaj

The nine margas or paths of bhakti yoga

Any of these nine paths will lead one to the Lord. There are examples in the scriptures, where each of these has been practised to perfection—Pariksit Maharaj, the grandson of Arjuna, who is the listener of Shrimad Bhagavatam is the epitome of sravanam, while the speaker, Sukadeva Goswami, the son of Veda Vyasa, is an embodiment of kirtanam. Prahlada is the illustration of smaranam as he remembered the holy name of the lord at all times, even when being burnt alive by his aunt Holika. Prthu Maharaj perfected archanam or worshipping the deity and Akrura is exemplary in vandanam or offering prayers. Lakshmi is noted for serving the feet of the Lord or pada-sevanam, while Hanuman's devotion to Rama demonstrates servitude or dasyam. Arjuna is sakha or a friend with Krishna and Bali signifies surrendering or atma-nivedanam when he tells Vamana avatar of Vishnu to rest his feet on his head.'

'Thank you so much for that detailed description of what yoga truly is. So which yoga is superior? Which one should we follow?' I asked.

'The one that appeals to you is superior for you. It is like asking which of the sciences is superior—physics, chemistry, biology or engineering. It depends on which aspect of science you like. Just like we have different types of scientists—physicists, chemists, biologists and engineers, we also have different types of spiritual scientists. The Bhagavad Gita (verses 13.25 and 13.26) say, "Some perceive the Super Soul within themselves through meditation, others through the cultivation of knowledge, and still others through working without fruitive desires. There are others who are unaware of these spiritual paths, but they hear from others and begin worshipping the Supreme Lord. By such devotion to hearing from saints, they too can gradually cross over the ocean of birth and death."

Gyana yogi may be viewed as a physicist as he is seeking impersonal Brahman and trying to understand the laws of nature just as a physicist tries to understand how the universe behaves by studying matter, energy and forces. The gyana yogi is seeking God through knowledge/wisdom and typically is a student of Upanishads. On the other hand, dhyana yogi is like a biologist focusing on the Paramatma inside the heart. Just as a biologist tries to understand the intricacies of what lies within the body as opposed to a physicist who is more interested in what lies beyond, the dhyana yogi is looking inside himself and searching for the Brahman within. Bhakti Yogi is like a chemist as he is seeking a personal loving relationship with God. We say love is chemistry. The bhakti yogi is looking for that chemistry between the self and the Brahman. Finally, the karma yogi is a doer and is engaged in action just as an engineer typically is building things. A true karma yogi does everything without any selfish motive—focuses on actions and not the results.

Just as you asked me which yoga is superior, in the Bhagavad Gita (Verse 2.7), Arjuna also asked the same question to Krishna as to what is the best for him, "Now I am confused about my duty and have lost all composure because of weakness. In this condition, I am asking you to tell me clearly what is best for me. Now I am your disciple, and a soul surrendered unto you. Please instruct me." Krishna advised Arjuna to be a yogi and walked him through different yoga systems.

About gyana yoga, Krishna mentions in the Verse 12.5: "For those whose minds are attached to the unmanifested, impersonal feature of the Supreme, advancement is very troublesome. To make progress in that discipline is always difficult for those who are embodied."

About dhyana yoga, Arjuna acknowledges in the Bhagavad Gita (verses 6.33 and 6.34): "The system of yoga which you have summarized appears impractical and unendurable to me, for the mind is unsteady. The mind is restless, turbulent, obstinate and very strong, and to subdue it, I think, is more difficult than controlling the wind."

About bhakti yoga Krishna mentions in the Bhagavad Gita (verses 7.16 and 7.17): "Typically four kinds of people worship God—the distressed (*aartha*), those who desire something (*artharthi*), the inquisitive (*jigyasu*), and the ones who are searching for knowledge of the Absolute (*gyani*). Of these, the one who is in full knowledge and who is always engaged in pure devotional service is the best. For I am very dear to him, and he is dear to me."

And in the Bhagavad Gita (Verse 3.30), Krishna tells Arjuna to be karma yogi as that was the path best suited for him—"O Arjuna, surrendering all your works unto me, with mind intent on me, and without desire for gain and free from egoism and lethargy, fight." He advises Arjuna to execute his duty as a soldier and fight.

The very last words uttered by Arjuna in the Bhagavad Gita are: "My dear Krishna, O infallible one, my illusion is now gone. I have regained my memory by your mercy, and I am now firm and free from doubt and am prepared to act according to your instructions."'

'Is that the last line of the Gita?' I asked.

WHAT IS GITA?

'Actually, it is not. While the Bhagavad Gita is a dialogue between Arjuna and Krishna, there are two more speakers in the Bhagavad Gita.'

'Who are they?' I inquired.

'Dhritarashtra and Sanjaya. Mahabharata's Kurukshetra war is essentially a war between two groups of cousins over the kingdom. The sons of Dhritarashtra known as the Kauravas were at war with the Pandavas, the sons of Dhitarashtra's brother Pandu. Dhritarashtra is the regent king of Hastinapur, who succeeded to the throne after his brother died leaving behind minor kids. The laws of succession demanded that Dhritarashtra, being a regent king, pass on the kingdom to his nephews. However, his eldest son felt that the kingdom belonged to his father, and saw himself as the rightful heir.

Contrary to the popular belief, the rules of succession at that time dictated that the most eligible son becomes the next king and not the eldest son. Dhritarashtra being blind was not deemed to be the most eligible person to rule. It was only after Pandu died an untimely death that Dhritarashtra became a regent king as all the sons of Pandu were too young to rule. When the Pandavas were mature enough to rule, Dhritarashtra's sons refused to even part with five villages, which was a very humble demand from the Pandavas, who were willing to relinquish the claim to the kingdom provided they were given five villages to rule.

When all negotiations failed, eventually a war ensued with armies of both the sides facing each other. Dhritarashtra being blind could not see the war but his charioteer Sanjaya was granted a boon to be able to see the war without actually being present at the battleground. The modern equivalent of that would be a CCTV camera. Sanjaya narrates the eyewitness account of the war to Dhritarashtra. The latter naturally wanting to know who will win the war asks, "O Sanjaya, after my sons and the sons of Pandu assembled in the place of pilgrimage at Kurukshetra, desiring to fight, what did they do?" This is the very first shloka of the Bhagavad Gita, a song of 700 shlokas, which itself is part of a much bigger book called Mahabharata which has about 100,000 shlokas. And in the last shloka of the Bhagavad Gita, Sanjaya answers Dhritarashtra's question, "Wherever there is Krishna, the master of all yogas, and wherever there is Arjuna, the supreme archer, there will also certainly be opulence, victory, extraordinary power and morality. That is my opinion."'

'My goodness! The Mahabharata is so big—100,000 shlokas!' I exclaimed.

'Yes, it is huge. It is compiled by Krishna Dvaipayana, who's name means "the dark one living on an island", who is also known as Veda Vyasa. Vyasa literally means compiler. So, Veda Vyasa was someone who compiled the veda. I had mentioned to you about various mahayugas. As you know we are currently in the twenty-eighth mahayuga of the seventh manvantara. The veda is divided into four in each mahayuga in Dwaparayuga. This is done because as yugas progress and we start to reach Kaliyuga, the human intelligence diminishes and life expectancy is reduced to only about 100 years. In contrast, people in Dwaparayuga lived about 1,000 years,

Tretayuga about 10,000 years and Satyayuga about 100,000 years.

Ravana, who lived in Tretayuga, sang hymns in praise of Shiva for 1,000 years or roughly one-tenth of the life expectancy in that yuga. Shiva finally blessed him and granted him an invincible sword and a powerful *linga* to worship. Rama was 28 when his 60,000 year-old father King Dasharatha had to send him into exile for 14 years. Upon his return, he is said to have ruled Ayodhya for 11,000 years before returning to vaikuntha. So, as you can see people in previous yugas are mentioned to have lived longer. It is important that just before another Kaliyuga comes, in which human life expectancy and intelligence shortens tremendously, someone divides the vedas into many parts for the benefit of the mankind. The one who does this task is given the title Veda Vyasa and is considered to be the literary incarnation of Vishnu.'

'Oh wow! So there have been many Veda Vyasas?'

'Yes of course, and there will be many more to come. Veda Vyasa is a post and not a person. Just like presidents and prime ministers change with time, Veda Vyasas also change with time. Veda means knowledge or wisdom and comes from the root word 'vid' which means to know. In fact, vedas are considered *apaurusheya* literally meaning 'of non-human origin'. The vedas are considered to be *svatah pramana* meaning "self-evident means of knowledge" which are true in themselves. Veda Vyasas are simply dividing this knowledge into four and not inventing it. The Vishnu Purana mentions all the 28 Veda Vyasas who have come until now in the current manvantara (one manvantara is a period of 30,67,20,000 years) and also the one who will be the next. The next Veda Vyasa in the 29th mahayuga cycle shall be

Aswathama who is the son of Dronacharya and is blessed to be *cheeranjeevi* meaning one with a very long life.

In Vishnu Purana Chapter 3, Maitreya asks Sage Parashara, who is the father of Krishna Dvaipayana or the current Veda Vyasa, "I have learnt from you, in due order, how this world is Vishnu; how it is in Vishnu; how it is from Vishnu: nothing further is to be known, but I should desire to hear how the vedas were divided, in different ages, by that great being, in the form of Veda Vyasa? Who were the Vyasas of their respective eras? And what were the branches into which the vedas were distributed?" To this Parashara replies, "The branches of the great tree of the vedas are so numerous, Maitreya, that it is impossible to describe them at length. I will give you a summarized account of them. In every Dwapara age, Vishnu appears as Vyasa, in order to promote the good of mankind, divides the veda, which is properly but one, into many portions: observing the limited perseverance, energy, and application of mortals, he makes the veda fourfold, to adapt it to their capacities; and the bodily form which he assumes, in order to effect that classification, is known by the name of Veda Vyasa.

Of the different Vyasas in the present manvantara, and the branches which they have taught, you shall have an account. Twenty eight times have the vedas been arranged by the great rishis in the Vaivaswata Manvantara in the Dwapara age, and consequently eight and twenty Vyasas have passed away; by whom, in their respective periods, the Veda has been divided into four. In the first Dwapara age, the distribution was made by Swayambhu (Brahma) himself; in the second, the arranger of the Veda (Veda Vyasa) was Prajapati (or Manu); in the third, Usanas; in the fourth, Vrihaspati; in the fifth,

Savitri; in the sixth, Mrityu (Death or Yama); in the seventh, Indra; in the eighth, Vasishtha; in the ninth, Saraswata; in the tenth, Tridhaman; in the eleventh, Trivrishan; in the twelfth, Bharadwaja; in the thirteenth, Antariksha; in the fourteenth, Vapra; in the fifteenth, Trayyaruna; in the sixteenth, Dhananjaya; in the seventeenth, Kritanjaya; in the eighteenth, Rina; in the nineteenth, Bharadwaja; in the twentieth, Gotama; in the twenty-first, Uttama, also called Haryatma; in the twenty-second, Vena, who is likewise named Rájaśravas; in the twenty-third, Somasushmapana, also Trinavindu; in the twenty-fourth, Riksha, the descendant of Bhrigu, who is also known by the name Valmiki; in the twenty-fifth, my father Sakti was the Vyasa; I was the Vyasa of the twenty-sixth Dwapara, and was succeeded by Jaratkaru; the Vyasa of the twenty-eighth, who followed him, was Krishna Dwaipayana... In the next Dwapara, Drauni (the son of Drona) will be the Vyasa, when my son, the Muni Krishna Dwaipayana, who is the current Vyasa, shall cease to be (in that character)."'

'What is the purpose of the vedas?' I asked.

Charan expounded, 'Vedas have three purposes—*Sambandha, Abhidheya* and *Prayojana*. Sambandha means understanding the connection between the Supreme Being, the material universe and the living entities. Prayojana means the ultimate goal, which is to establish this connection and abhidheya means the process of establishing this sambandha or connection.'

'So, all the Vyasas were working towards these three goals?' I chipped in.

Charan continued, 'Yes and some Vyasas were more enthusiastic than others. They did much more than just divide the vedas. For example, Valmiki wrote the Ramayana in addition to splitting the vedas. Similarly, Krishna Dwaipayana, the current Veda Vyasa, wrote Bhagavata Purana and also the Mahabharata. The Bhagavad Gita itself is a part of the Mahabharata which has many other gitas or songs in it, such as Anu Gita, Vyadha Gita, Uddhava Gita etc. Actually, technically it is a bit incorrect to say Krishna is speaking to Arjuna in the Bhagavad Gita.'

'It is incorrect?' I asked in disbelief!

'It depends on how you look at it. In the absolute sense, Sauti is saying it.'

'Who is Sauti?' I wondered.

'The book Mahabharata actually begins with a character called Sauti coming to a group of sages or rishis, who ask him where he had been? Sauti says that he was at the snake sacrifice ceremony of King Janamejaya, the son of Pariskhit (grandson of Arjuna, son of Abhimanyu) where Vaishampayana was telling the tales of the Mahabharata composed by Veda Vyasa or Krishna Dvaipayana. So, in reality, Sauti is telling what he heard from Vaishampayana, who in turn is telling what was composed by Veda Vyasa. In this narration, Sauti tells what Sanajya heard Krishna say. So, it is actually four levels of narrations—Veda Vyasa, the compiler of the Mahabharata, through Sanjaya telling what Krishna said to Arjuna, which was narrated by Vaishampayana and now being retold by Sauti! And if that was not complicated enough, picture this—it is actually as if Veda Vyasa or Krishna Dwaipayana, the author, quoting his own book in the very book he is writing!'

'Wow! I am amazed at the maze of the narrations there. The Mahabharata really seems epic,' I smiled at the double meaning of epic.

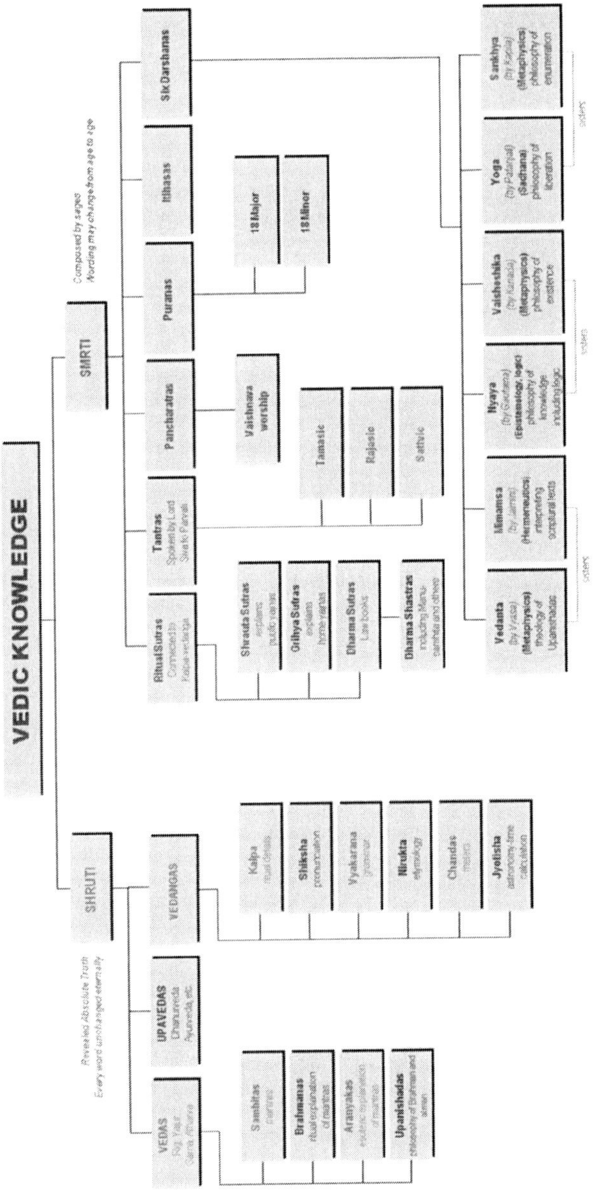
VEDIC KNOWLEDGE
SHRUTI
Revealed Absolute Truth
Every word unchanged eternally
SMRTI
Composed by sages
Wording may change from age to age
VEDAS
UPAVEDAS
VEDANGAS
Samhitas
Brahmanas
Aranyakas
Upanishadas
Kalpa
Shiksha
Vyakarana
Nirukta
Chandas
Jyotisha
Ritual Sutras
Tantras
Pancharatras
Puranas
Itihasas
Six Darshanas
Shrauta Sutras
Grihya Sutras
Dharma Sutras
Law books
Dharma Shastras
Tamasic
Rajasic
Vaishnava worship
18 Major
18 Minor
Vedanta
Mimamsa
Nyaya
Vaisheshika
Yoga
Sankhya
sisters
sisters
sisters

'And the Mahabharata itself is a drop in the ocean of vedic scriptures,' Charan said while showing me a picture on his phone.

'This is so huge! But I can't see the Mahabharata and the Gita mentioned anywhere on this,' I wondered.

'That is because this chart is too small to show individual books such as the Mahabharata or the Ramayana. Both are classified as Itihasa which when broken down is 'iti-ha-sa' meaning "this has happened" or in other words history. A cousin of Itihasa is Purana which means something which happened a long time ago. So, in colloquial language that would mean ancient history as opposed to Itihasas which would be more like recent history. As you can see Itihasas and Puranas are mentioned under Smrti,' Charan says zooming in on the image.

'What is Smrti?' I asked.

'Vedic scriptures are largely divided into two—Shruti and Smrti. Shruti means what you hear and smrti means what you remember. The scriptures classified as Shruti are passed down generations in a tradition of word-for-word recitation while Smrti was composed by sages and words may change here and there as they do not have as rigorous a system of oral recitation and retention as Shruti does. Vedas are Shruti while Itihasas such as the Mahabharata and the Ramayana are Smrti.'

'Why could they not just write it down on paper and then it would be the same word-for-word?'

Charan smiles and says, 'Paper is a relatively recent invention, so it is not as easy as you think. In fact, before paper came into being these shlokas were written on leaves. And as you know leaves have a limited shelf life. It is indeed amazing how Vedas have been passed down largely orally from time immemorial as Shruti.'

I acknowledged and asked, 'But then what makes the Bhagavad Gita so great? As I can see from your chart, the volume of vedic scriptures is massive while the Bhagavad Gita is only 700 shlokas.'

'Excellent question! These 700 shlokas of the Bhagavad Gita that appear from Chapter 25 to Chapter 42 of 'Bhisma Parva' section of the 100,000-shloka-long Mahabharata, which itself is a drop in the ocean, is indeed the summary of the Vedic knowledge. The magnificence of the Bhagavad Gita is captured in the Bhagavad Gita Mahatmya, written by the Indian Philosopher Adi Shankaracharya, meaning 'Glories of the Bhagavad Gita'. It is a conversation between Lord Shiva and his consort Parvati. Lord Shiva praises the Bhagavad Gita:

sarvo panishado gaavo dogdha gopala nandanah
partho vatsah srutir bhoktah dugdham gitamrtam mahat

It means, "All the Upanishads are cows; the milker is Gopala Nanda, the cowherd boy (i.e., Krishna); Partha (i.e., Arjuna) is the calf; men of purified intellect are the drinkers, and the milk is the great nectar of the Gita." The Bhagavad Gita is also called 'Geetopanishad' and is considered the essence of all Upanishads and scriptures. Thus, if one studies the Bhagavad Gita, it is as good as knowing the essence of all scriptures.'

'I am totally convinced that the Bhagavad Gita is indeed the summary of the Vedic knowledge. You helped me clear my misunderstandings of so many concepts such as dharma, karma, yoga and Bhagavan. I am amazed at how much these 700 shlokas contain. I must take your leave now,' I said as I looked at my watch which showed 7.23 p.m.

Just as I said this and was booking a cab on my mobile, Charan came up to me and said, 'Here, take this book. It will help you.'

I was totally mesmerized by that gesture as I held the rather old and somewhat worn-out book in my hands. My cab arrived in about three minutes. As I sat inside, I opened the first page which had something scribbled on it. I kept reading until I came to the last line which read, 'From Dharma Thakur to Charan Saket–28 May 1997'. I went back to the first line and it said, 'From Gyana Chanda to Adhyatma Sirohi—18 Jan 1870'. Suddenly it dawned upon me that he had given me a more than 150-year-old book! Probably that is how paramapara works I thought as I scribbled, 'From Saket Charan to Anveshak Jigyanshu–30 August 2021'.

APPENDIX*

(MODERN PROBLEMS, ANCIENT SOLUTIONS)

*The shlokas mentioned in this appendix are taken from https://vedabase.io/.

Find solutions to your problems in the Bhagavad Gita

Anger
Chapter 2 - Shloka 56
Chapter 2 - Shloka 62
Chapter 2 - Shloka 63
Chapter 5 - Shloka 26
Chapter 16 - Shlokas 1-3
Chapter 16 - Shloka 21

Confusion
Chapter 2 - Shloka 7
Chapter 3 - Shloka 2
Chapter 18 - Shloka 61

Death
Chapter 2 - Shloka 13
Chapter 2 - Shloka 20
Chapter 2 - Shloka 22
Chapter 2 - Shloka 25
Chapter 2 - Shloka 27

Demotivation
Chapter 11 - Shloka 33
Chapter 18 - Shloka 48
Chapter 18 - Shloka 78

Depression
Chapter 2 - Shloka 3
Chapter 2 - Shloka 14
Chapter 5 - Shloka 21

Discrimination
Chapter 5 - Shloka 18
Chapter 5 - Shloka 19
Chapter 6 - Shloka 32
Chapter 9 - Shloka 29

Envy
Chapter 12 - Shlokas 13-14
Chapter 16 - Shloka 19
Chapter 18 - Shloka 71

Fear
Chapter 4 - Shloka 10
Chapter 11 - Shloka 50
Chapter 18 - Shloka 30

Feeling Sinful
Chapter 4 - Shloka 36
Chapter 4 - Shloka 37
Chapter 5 - Shloka 10
Chapter 9 - Shloka 30
Chapter 10 - Shloka 3
Chapter 14 - Shloka 6
Chapter 18 - Shloka 66

Forgetfulness
Chapter 15 - Shloka 15
Chapter 18 - Shloka 61

Forgiveness
Cahpter 11 - Shloka 44
Chapter 12 - Shlokas 13-14
Chapter 16 - Shlokas 1-3

Greed
Cahpter 14 - Shloka 17
Chapter 16 - Shloka 21
Chapter 17 - Shloka 25

Laziness
Chapter 3 - Shloka 8
Chapter 3 - Shloka 20
Chapter 6 - Shloka 16
Chapter 18 - Shloka 39

Loneliness
Chapter 6 - Shloka 30
Chapter 9 - Shloka 29
Chapter 13 - Shloka 16
Chapter 13 - Shloka 18

Losing Hope
Chapter 4 - Shloka 11
Chapter 9 - Shloka 22
Chapter 9 - Shloka 34
Chapter 18 - Shloka 66
Chapter 18 - Shloka 78

Lust
Chapter 3 - Shloka 37
Chapter 3 - Shloka 41
Chapter 3 - Shloka 43
Chapter 5 - Shloka 22
Chapter 16 - Shloka 21

Pride
Chapter 16- Shloka 4
Chapter 16 - Shlokas 13-15
Chapter 18 - Shloka 26
Chapter 18 - Shloka 58

Seeking Peace
Chapter 2 - Shloka 66
Chapter 2 - Shloka 71
Chapter 4 - Shloka 39
Chapter 5 - Shloka 29
Chapter 8 - Shloka 28

Temptation
Chapter 2 - Shloka 60
Chapter 2 - Shloka 61
Chapter 2 - Shloka 70
Chapter 7 - Shloka 14

Uncontrolled Mind
Chapter 6 - Shloka 5
Chapter 6 - Shloka 6
Chapter 6 - Shloka 26
Chapter 6 - Shloka 35

ANGER

- Shloka 2.56

duḥkheṣv anudvigna-manāḥsukheṣu vigata-spṛhaḥ
vīta-rāga-bhaya-krodhaḥsthita-dhīr munir ucyate

One who is not disturbed in mind even amidst the threefold miseries or elated when there is happiness, and who is free from attachment, fear and anger, is called a sage of steady mind.

- Shloka 2.62

dhyāyato viṣayān puṁsaḥsaṅgas teṣūpajāyate
saṅgāt sañjāyate kāmaḥkāmāt krodho 'bhijāyate

While contemplating the objects of the senses, a person develops attachment for them, and from such attachment lust develops, and from lust arises anger.

- Shloka 2.63

krodhād bhavati sammohaḥsammohāt smṛti-vibhramaḥ
smṛti-bhraṁśād buddhi-nāśobuddhi-nāśāt praṇaśyati

From anger, complete delusion arises, and from delusion bewilderment of memory. When memory is bewildered, intelligence is lost, and when intelligence is lost one falls down again into the material pool.

- Shloka 5.26

kāma-krodha-vimuktānāṁ yatīnāṁ yata-cetasām
abhito brahma-nirvāṇaṁ vartate viditātmanām

Those who are free from anger and all material desires, who are self-realized, self-disciplined and constantly endeavouring for perfection, are assured of liberation in the Supreme in the very near future.

- Shlokas 16.1–3

abhayaṁ sattva-sanśhuddhir jñāna-yoga-vyavasthitiḥ
dānaṁ damaśh cha yajñaśh cha svādhyāyas tapa ārjavam
ahinsā satyam akrodhas tyāgaḥ śhāntir apaiśhunam
dayā bhūteṣhv aloluptvaṁ mārdavaṁ hrīr achāpalam
tejaḥ kṣhamā dhṛitiḥ śhaucham adroho nāti-mānitā
bhavanti sampadaṁ daivīm abhijātasya bhārata

Fearlessness; purification of one's existence; cultivation of spiritual knowledge; charity; self-control; performance of sacrifice; study of the Vedas; austerity; simplicity; non-violence; truthfulness; freedom from anger; renunciation; tranquillity; aversion to fault-finding; compassion for all living entities; freedom from covetousness; gentleness; modesty; steady determination; vigour; forgiveness; fortitude; cleanliness; and freedom from envy and from the passion for honor—these transcendental qualities, O son of Bharata, belong to godly men endowed with divine nature.

- Shloka 16.21

tri-vidhaṁ narakasyedaṁ dvāraṁ nāśanam ātmanaḥ
kāmaḥ krodhas tathā lobhas tasmād etat trayaṁ tyajet

There are three gates leading to this hell—lust, anger and greed. Every sane person should give these up for they lead to the degradation of the soul.

CONFUSION

- Shloka 2.7

kārpaṇya-doṣopahata-svabhāvaḥpṛcchāmi tvāṁ
dharma-sammūḍha-cetāḥ
yac chreyaḥ syān niścitaṁ brūhi tan meśiṣyas
te 'haṁ śādhi māṁ tvāṁ prapannam

Now I am confused about my duty and have lost all composure because of miserly weakness. In this condition I am asking You to tell me for certain what is best for me. Now I am Your disciple and a soul surrendered unto You. Please instruct me.

- Shloka 3.2

vyāmiśreṇeva vākyena buddhiṁ mohayasīva me
tad ekaṁ vada niścitya yena śreyo 'ham āpnuyām

My intelligence is bewildered by Your equivocal instructions. Therefore, please tell me decisively which will be most beneficial for me.

- Shloka 18.61

īśvaraḥ sarva-bhūtānāṁ hṛd-deśe 'rjuna tiṣṭhati
bhrāmayan sarva-bhūtāni yantrārūḍhāni māyayā

The Supreme Lord is situated in everyone's heart, O Arjuna, and is directing the wanderings of all living entities, who are seated as on a machine, made of the material energy.

DEATH

- Shloka 2.13

dehino 'smin yathā dehe kaumāraṁ yauvanaṁ jarā
tathā dehāntara-prāptir dhīras tatra na muhyati

As the embodied soul continuously passes, in this body, from boyhood to youth to old age, the soul similarly passes into another body at death. A sober person is not bewildered by such a change.

- Shloka 2.20

na jāyate mriyate vā kadācin nāyaṁ
bhūtvā bhavitā vā na bhūyaḥ
ajo nityaḥ śāśvato 'yaṁ purāṇo
na hanyate hanyamāne śarīre

For the soul, there is neither birth nor death at any time. He has not come into being, does not come into being, and will not come into being. He is unborn, eternal, ever-existing and primeval. He is not slain when the body is slain.

- Shloka 2.22

vāsāṁsi jīrṇāni yathā vihāya navāni gṛhṇāti naro 'parāṇi
tathā śarīrāṇi vihāya jīrṇāny anyāni saṁyāti navāni dehī

As a person puts on new garments, giving up old ones, the soul similarly accepts new material bodies, giving up the old and useless ones.

- Shloka 2.25

avyakto 'yam acintyo 'yam avikāryo 'yam ucyate
tasmād evaṁ viditvainaṁ nānuśocitum arhasi

It is said that the soul is invisible, inconceivable and immutable. Knowing this, you should not grieve for the body.

- Shloka 2.27

jātasya hi dhruvo mṛtyur dhruvaṁ janma mṛtasya ca
tasmād aparihārye 'rthe na tvaṁ śocitum arhasi

One who has taken his birth is sure to die, and after death one is sure to take birth again. Therefore, in the unavoidable discharge of your duty, you should not lament.

DEMOTIVATION

- Shloka 11.33

tasmāt tvam uttiṣṭha yaśo labhasva jitvā
śatrūn bhuṅkṣva rājyaṁ samṛddham
mayaivaite nihatāḥ pūrvam eva
nimitta-mātraṁ bhava savya-sācin

Therefore get up. Prepare to fight and win glory. Conquer your enemies and enjoy a flourishing kingdom. They are already put to death by My arrangement, and you, O Savyasaci, can be but an instrument in the fight.

- Shloka 18.48

saha-jaṁ karma kaunteya sa-doṣam api na tyajet
sarvārambhā hi doṣeṇa dhūmenāgnir ivāvṛtāḥ

Every endeavour is covered by some fault, just as fire is covered by smoke. Therefore one should not give up the work born of his nature, O son of Kunti, even if such work is full of fault.

- Shloka 18.78

yatra yogeśvaraḥ kṛṣṇo yatra pārtho dhanur-dharaḥ
tatra śrīr vijayo bhūtir dhruvā nītir matir mama

Wherever there is Krishna, the master of all mystics, and wherever there is Arjuna, the supreme archer, there will also certainly be opulence, victory, extraordinary power and morality. That is my opinion.

DEPRESSION

- Shloka 2.3

klaibyaṁ mā sma gamaḥ pārtha naitat tvayy upapadyate
kṣudraṁ hṛdaya-daurbalyaṁ tyaktvottiṣṭha paran-tapa

O son of Pṛthā, do not yield to this degrading impotence. It does not become you. Give up such petty weakness of heart and arise, O chastiser of the enemy.

- Shloka 2.14

mātrā-sparśās tu kaunteya śītoṣṇa-sukha-duḥkha-dāḥ
āgamāpāyino 'nityās tāṁs titikṣasva bhārata

O son of Kunti, the non-permanent appearance of happiness and distress and their disappearance in due course are like the appearance and disappearance of winter and summer seasons. They arise from sense perception, O scion of Bharata, and one must learn to tolerate them without being disturbed.

- Shloka 5.21

bāhya-sparśeṣv asaktātmā vindaty ātmani yat sukham
sa brahma-yoga-yuktātmā sukham akṣayam aśnute

Such a liberated person is not attracted to material sense pleasure but is always in trance, enjoying the pleasure within. In this way the self-realized person enjoys unlimited happiness, for he concentrates on the Supreme.

DISCRIMINATION

- Shloka 5.18

vidyā-vinaya-sampanne brāhmaṇe gavi hastini
śuni caiva śva-pāke ca paṇḍitāḥ sama-darśinaḥ

The humble sages, by virtue of true knowledge, see with equal vision a learned and gentle Brahmin, a cow, an elephant, a dog and a dog-eater [outcaste].

- Shloka 5.19

ihaiva tair jitaḥ sargo yeṣāṁ sāmye sthitaṁ manaḥ
nirdoṣaṁ hi samaṁ brahma tasmād brahmaṇi te sthitāḥ

Those whose minds are established in sameness and equanimity have already conquered the conditions of birth and death. They are flawless like Brahman and thus they are already situated in Brahman.

- Shloka 6.32

ātmaupamyena sarvatra samaṁ paśyati yo 'rjuna
sukhaṁ vā yadi vā duḥkhaṁ sa yogī paramo mataḥ

He is a perfect yogi who, by comparison to his own self, sees the true equality of all beings, in both their happiness and their distress, O Arjuna!

- Shloka 9.29

samo 'haṁ sarva-bhūteṣu na me dveṣyo 'sti na priyaḥ
ye bhajanti tu māṁ bhaktyā mayi te teṣu cāpy aham

I envy no one, nor am I partial to anyone. I am equal to all. But whoever renders service unto Me in devotion is a friend, is in Me, and I am also a friend to him.

ENVY

- Shlokas 12.13-14

adveṣṭā sarva-bhūtānāṁ maitraḥ karuṇa eva ca
nirmamo nirahaṅkāraḥ sama-duḥkha-sukhaḥ kṣamī
santuṣṭaḥ satataṁ yogī yatātmā dṛḍha-niścayaḥ
mayy arpita-mano-buddhir yo mad-bhaktaḥ sa me priyaḥ

One who is not envious but is a kind friend to all living entities, who does not think himself a proprietor and is free from false ego, who is equal in both happiness and distress, who is tolerant, always satisfied, self-controlled, and engaged in devotional service with determination, his mind and intelligence fixed on Me—such a devotee of Mine is very dear to Me.

- Shloka 16.19

tān ahaṁ dviṣataḥ krūrān saṁsāreṣu narādhamān
kṣipāmy ajasram aśubhān āsurīṣv eva yoniṣu

Those who are envious and mischievous, who are the lowest among men, I perpetually cast into the ocean of material existence, into various demoniac species of life.

- Shloka 18.71

śraddhāvān anasūyaś ca śṛṇuyād api yo naraḥ
so 'pi muktaḥ śubhāl̲ lokān prāpnuyāt puṇya-karmaṇām

And one who listens with faith and without envy becomes free from sinful reactions and attains to the auspicious planets where the pious dwell.

FEAR

- Shloka 4.10

vīta-rāga-bhaya-krodhā man-mayā mām upāśritāḥ
bahavo jñāna-tapasā pūtā mad-bhāvam āgatāḥ

Being freed from attachment, fear and anger, being fully absorbed in Me and taking refuge in Me, many, many persons in the past became purified by knowledge of Me—and thus they all attained transcendental love for Me.

- Shloka 11.50

sañjaya uvāca
ity arjunaṁ vāsudevas tathoktvā svakaṁ rūpaṁ darśayām āsa bhūyaḥ āśvāsayām āsa ca bhītam enaṁ bhūtvā punaḥ saumya-vapur mahatma

Sanjaya said to Dhritarashtra: Krishna, having spoken thus to Arjuna, displayed His real four-armed form and at last showed His two-armed form, thus encouraging the fearful Arjuna.

- Shloka 18.30

pravṛttiṁ ca nivṛttiṁ ca kāryākārye bhayābhaye
bandhaṁ mokṣaṁ ca yā vetti buddhiḥ sā pārtha sāttvikī

O son of Pṛthā, that understanding by which one knows what ought to be done and what ought not to be done, what is to be feared and what is not to be feared, what is binding and what is liberating, is in the mode of goodness.

FEELING SINFUL

- Shlokas 4.36

> api ced asi pāpebhyaḥ sarvebhyaḥ pāpa-kṛt-tamaḥ
> sarvaṁ jñāna-plavenaiva vṛjinaṁ santariṣyasi

Even if you are considered to be the most sinful of all sinners, when you are situated in the boat of transcendental knowledge you will be able to cross over the ocean of miseries.

- Shlokas 4.37

> yathaidhāṁsi samiddho 'gnir bhasma-sāt kurute 'rjuna
> jñānāgniḥ sarva-karmāṇi bhasma-sāt kurute tathā

As a blazing fire turns firewood to ashes, O Arjuna, so does the fire of knowledge burns to ashes all reactions to material activities.

- Shlokas 5.10

> brahmaṇy ādhāya karmāṇi saṅgaṁ tyaktvā karoti yaḥ
> lipyate na sa pāpena padma-patram ivāmbhasā

One who performs his duty without attachment, surrendering the results unto the Supreme Lord, is unaffected by sinful action, as the lotus leaf is untouched by water.

- Shloka 9.30

  api cet su-durācāro bhajate mām ananya-bhāk
  sādhur eva sa mantavyaḥ samyag vyavasito hi saḥ

Even if one commits the most abominable action, if he is engaged in devotional service he is to be considered saintly because he is properly situated in his determination.

- Shloka 10.3

  yo mām ajam anādiṁ ca vetti loka-maheśvaram
  asammūḍhaḥ sa martyeṣu sarva-pāpaiḥ pramucyate

He who knows Me as the unborn, as the beginningless, as the Supreme Lord of all the worlds—he only, undeluded among men, is freed from all sins.

- Shloka 14.6

  tatra sattvaṁ nirmalatvāt prakāśakam anāmayam
  sukha-saṅgena badhnāti jñāna-saṅgena cānagha

O sinless one, the mode of goodness, being purer than the others, is illuminating, and it frees one from all sinful reactions. Those situated in that mode become conditioned by a sense of happiness and knowledge.

- Shloka 18.66

  sarva-dharmān parityajya mām ekaṁ śaraṇaṁ vraja
  ahaṁ tvāṁ sarva-pāpebhyo mokṣayiṣyāmi mā śucaḥ

Abandon all varieties of religion and just surrender unto Me. I shall deliver you from all sinful reactions. Do not fear.

FORGETFULNESS

- Shloka 15.15

sarvasya cāhaṁ hṛdi sanniviṣṭo mattaḥ
smṛtir jñānam apohanaṁ ca
vedaiś ca sarvair aham eva vedyo
vedānta-kṛd veda-vid eva cāham

I am seated in everyone's heart, and from Me come remembrance, knowledge and forgetfulness. By all the vedas, I am to be known. Indeed, I am the compiler of vedanta, and I am the knower of the vedas.

- Shloka 18.61

īśvaraḥ sarva-bhūtānāṁ hṛd-deśe 'rjuna tiṣṭhati
bhrāmayan sarva-bhūtāni yantrārūḍhāni māyayā

The Supreme Lord is situated in everyone's heart, O Arjuna, and is directing the wanderings of all living entities, who are seated as on a machine, made of the material energy.

FORGIVENESS

- Shloka 11.44

tasmāt praṇamya praṇidhāya kāyaṁ
prasādaye tvām aham īśam īḍyam
piteva putrasya sakheva sakhyuḥ
priyaḥ priyāyārhasi deva soḍhum

You are the Supreme Lord, to be worshiped by every living being. Thus I fall down to offer You my respectful obeisances and ask Your mercy. As a father tolerates the impudence of his son, a friend the impertinence of a friend, or a husband the familiarity of his wife, please tolerate the wrongs I may have done You.

GREED

- Shloka 14.17

sattvāt sañjāyate jñānaṁ rajaso lobha eva ca
pramāda-mohau tamaso bhavato 'jñānam eva ca

From the mode of goodness, real knowledge develops; from the mode of passion, greed develops; and from the mode of ignorance develops foolishness, madness and illusion.

- Shloka 17.25

tad ity anabhisandhāyaphalaṁ yajña-tapaḥ-kriyāḥ
dāna-kriyāś ca vividhāḥkriyante mokṣa-kāṅkṣibhiḥ

Without desiring fruitive results, one should perform various kinds of sacrifice, penance and charity with the word tat. The purpose of such transcendental activities is to get free from material entanglement.

LAZINESS

- Shloka 3.8

niyataṁ kuru karma tvaṁ karma jyāyo hy akarmaṇaḥ
śarīra-yātrāpi ca te na prasidhyed akarmaṇaḥ

Perform your prescribed duty, for doing so is better than not working. One cannot even maintain one's physical body without work.

- Shloka 3.20

karmaṇaiva hi saṁsiddhim āsthitā janakādayaḥ
loka-saṅgraham evāpi sampaśyan kartum arhasi

Kings such as Janaka attained perfection solely by performance of prescribed duties. Therefore, just for the sake of educating the people in general, you should perform your work.

- Shloka 6.16

nāty-aśnatas tu yogo 'sti na caikāntam anaśnataḥ
na cāti-svapna-śīlasya jāgrato naiva cārjuna

There is no possibility of one becoming a yogi, O Arjuna, if one eats too much or eats too little, sleeps too much or does not sleep enough.

- Shloka 18.39

yad agre cānubandhe ca sukhaṁ mohanam ātmanaḥ
nidrālasya-pramādotthaṁ tat tāmasam udāhṛtam

And that happiness which is blind to self-realization, which is delusional from beginning to end and which arises from sleep, laziness and illusion is said to be of the nature of ignorance.

LONELINESS

- Shloka 6.30

yo māṁ paśyati sarvatra sarvaṁ ca mayi paśyati
tasyāhaṁ na praṇaśyāmi sa ca me na praṇaśyati

For one who sees Me everywhere and sees everything in Me, I am never lost, nor is he ever lost to Me.

- Shloka 13.16

bahir antaś ca bhūtānām acaraṁ caram eva ca
sūkṣmatvāt tad avijñeyaṁ dūra-sthaṁ cāntike ca tat

The Supreme Truth exists outside and inside of all living beings, the moving and the non-moving. Because He is subtle, He is beyond the power of the material senses to see or to know. Although far, far away, He is also near to all.

- Shloka 13.18

jyotiṣām api taj jyotis tamasaḥ param ucyate
jñānaṁ jñeyaṁ jñāna-gamyaṁ hṛdi sarvasya viṣṭhitam

He is the source of light in all luminous objects. He is beyond the darkness of matter and is unmanifested. He is knowledge, He is the object of knowledge, and He is the goal of knowledge. He is situated in everyone's heart.

LOSING HOPE

- Shloka 4.11

ye yathā māṁ prapadyante tāṁs tathaiva bhajāmy aham
mama vartmānuvartante manuṣyāḥ pārtha sarvaśaḥ

As all surrender unto Me, I reward them accordingly. Everyone follows My path in all respects, O son of Pṛthā.

- Shloka 9.22

ananyāś cintayanto māṁ ye janāḥ paryupāsate
teṣāṁ nityābhiyuktānāṁ yoga-kṣemaṁ vahāmy aham

But those who always worship Me with exclusive devotion, meditating on My transcendental form—to them I carry what they lack, and I preserve what they have.

- Shloka 9.34

man-manā bhava mad-bhakto mad-yājī māṁ namaskuru
mām evaiṣyasi yuktvaivam ātmānaṁ mat-parāyaṇaḥ

Engage your mind always in thinking of Me, become My devotee, offer obeisances to Me and worship Me. Being completely absorbed in Me, surely you will come to Me.

- Shloka 18.66

sarva-dharmān parityajya mām ekaṁ śaraṇaṁ vraja
ahaṁ tvāṁ sarva-pāpebhyo mokṣayiṣyāmi mā śucaḥ

Abandon all varieties of religion and just surrender unto Me. I shall deliver you from all sinful reactions. Do not fear.

LUST

- Shloka 3.37

kāma eṣa krodha eṣa rajo-guṇa-samudbhavaḥ
mahāśano mahā-pāpmā viddhy enam iha vairiṇam

It is lust only, Arjuna, which is born of contact with the material mode of passion and later transformed into wrath and which is the all-devouring sinful enemy of this world.

- Shloka 3.41

tasmāt tvam indriyāṇy ādau niyamya bharatarṣabha
pāpmānaṁ prajahi hy enaṁ jñāna-vijñāna-nāśanam

Therefore, O Arjuna, best of the Bharatas, in the very beginning curb this great symbol of sin [lust] by regulating the senses and slay this destroyer of knowledge and self-realization.

- Shloka 3.43

evaṁ buddheḥ paraṁ buddhvā saṁstabhyātmānam ātmanā
jahi śatruṁ mahā-bāho kāma-rūpaṁ durāsadam

Thus knowing oneself to be transcendental to the material senses, mind and intelligence, O mighty-armed Arjuna, one should steady the mind by deliberate spiritual intelligence and thus—by spiritual strength—conquer this insatiable enemy known as lust.

- Shloka 5.22

ye hi saṁsparśa-jā bhogā duḥkha-yonaya eva te
ādy-antavantaḥ kaunteya na teṣu ramate budhaḥ

An intelligent person does not take part in the sources of misery, which are due to contact with the material senses. O son of Kunti, such pleasures have a beginning and an end, and so the wise person does not delight in them.

PRIDE

- Shloka 16.4

dambho darpo 'bhimānaś ca krodhaḥ pāruṣyam eva ca
ajñānaṁ cābhijātasya pārtha sampadam āsurīm

Pride, arrogance, conceit, anger, harshness and ignorance—these qualities belong to those of demoniac nature, O son of Pṛthā.

- Shlokas 16.13-15

idam adya mayā labdham imaṁ prāpsye manoratham
idam astīdam api me bhaviṣhyati punar dhanam
asau mayā hataḥ śhatrur haniṣhye chāparān api
īśhvaro 'ham ahaṁ bhogī siddho 'haṁ balavān sukhī
āḍhyo 'bhijanavān asmi ko 'nyo 'sti sadṛiśho mayā
yakṣhye dāsyāmi modiṣhya ity ajñāna-vimohitāḥ

The demoniac person thinks: 'So much wealth do I have today, and I will gain more according to my schemes. So much is mine now, and it will increase in the future, more and more. He is my enemy, and I have killed him and my other enemies will also be killed. I am the lord of everything. I am the enjoyer. I am perfect, powerful and happy. I am the richest man, surrounded by aristocratic relatives. There is none so powerful and happy as I am. I shall perform sacrifices, I shall give some charity, and thus I shall rejoice.' In this way, such persons are deluded by ignorance.

- Shloka 18.26

mukta-saṅgo 'nahaṁ-vādī dhṛty-utsāha-samanvitaḥ
siddhy-asiddhyor nirvikāraḥ kartā sāttvika ucyate

One who performs his duty sans association with the modes of material nature, without false ego, with great determination and enthusiasm and without wavering in success or failure is said to be a worker in the mode of goodness.

- Shloka 18.58

mac-cittaḥ sarva-durgāṇi mat-prasādāt tariṣyasi
atha cet tvam ahaṅkārān na śroṣyasi vinaṅkṣyasi

If you become conscious of Me, you will pass over all the obstacles of conditioned life by My grace. If, however, you do not work in such consciousness but act through false ego, not hearing Me, you will be lost.

SEEKING PEACE

- Shloka 2.66

nāsti buddhir ayuktasya na cāyuktasya bhāvanā
na cābhāvayataḥ śāntir aśāntasya kutaḥ sukham

One who is not connected with the Supreme can have neither transcendental intelligence nor a steady mind, without which there is no possibility of peace. And how can there be any happiness without peace?

- Shloka 2.71

vihāya kāmān yaḥ sarvān pumāṁś carati niḥspṛhaḥ
nirmamo nirahaṅkāraḥ sa śāntim adhigacchati

A person who has given up all desires for sense gratification, who lives free from desires, who has given up all sense of proprietorship and is devoid of false ego, he alone can attain real peace.

- Shloka 4.39

śraddhāvāl̲ labhate jñānaṁ tat-paraḥ saṁyatendriyaḥ
jñānaṁ labdhvā parāṁ śāntim acireṇādhigacchati

A faithful person who is dedicated to transcendental knowledge and who subdues his senses is eligible to achieve it and having achieved it, he attains the supreme spiritual peace.

- Shloka 5.29

bhoktāraṁ yajña-tapasāṁ sarva-loka-maheśvaram
suhṛdaṁ sarva-bhūtānāṁ jñātvā māṁ śāntim ṛcchati

A person in full consciousness of Me, knowing Me to be the ultimate beneficiary of all sacrifices and austerities, the Supreme Lord of all planets and demigods and the benefactor and well-wisher of all living entities attains peace from the pangs of material miseries.

- Shloka 8.28

vedeṣu yajñeṣu tapaḥsu caiva dāneṣu
yat puṇya-phalaṁ pradiṣṭam
atyeti tat sarvam idaṁ viditvā yogī
paraṁ sthānam upaiti cādyam

A person who accepts the path of devotional service is not bereft of the results derived from studying the vedas, performing sacrifices, undergoing austerities, giving charity or pursuing philosophical and fruitive activities at all. Simply by performing devotional service, he attains all of these, and at the end he then reaches the supreme eternal abode.

TEMPTATION

- Shloka 2.60

yatato hy api kaunteya puruṣasya vipaścitaḥ
indriyāṇi pramāthīni haranti prasabhaṁ manaḥ

The senses are so strong and impetuous, O Arjuna, that they forcibly carry away the mind even of a person of discrimination who is endeavoring to control them.

- Shloka 2.61

> tāni sarvāṇi saṁyamya yukta āsīta mat-paraḥ
> vaśe hi yasyendriyāṇi tasya prajñā pratiṣṭhitā

One who restrains his senses, keeping them under full control, and fixes his consciousness upon Me, is known as a person of steady intelligence.

- Shloka 2.70

> āpūryamāṇam acala-pratiṣṭhaṁ
> samudram āpaḥ praviśanti yadvat
> tadvat kāmā yaṁ praviśanti sarve
> sa śāntim āpnoti na kāma-kāmī

A person who is not disturbed by the incessant flow of desires—that enter like rivers into the ocean, which is ever being filled but is always still—can alone achieve peace, and not the person who strives to satisfy such desires.

- Shloka 7.14

> *daivī hy eṣā guṇa-mayī mama māyā duratyayā*
> *mām eva ye prapadyante māyām etāṁ taranti te*

Bhagavad Gita 7.14

This divine energy of Mine, consisting of the three modes of material nature, is difficult to overcome. But those who have surrendered unto Me can easily cross beyond it.

UNCONTROLLED MIND

- Shloka 6.5

uddhared ātmanātmānaṁ nātmānam avasādayet
ātmaiva hy ātmano bandhur ātmaiva ripur ātmanaḥ

One must deliver himself with the help of his mind and not degrade himself. The mind is the friend of the conditioned soul and his enemy as well.

- Shloka 6.6

bandhur ātmātmanas tasya yenātmaivātmanā jitaḥ
anātmanas tu śatrutve vartetātmaiva śatru-vat

For him who has conquered the mind, the mind is the best of friends; but for one who has failed to do so, his mind will remain the greatest enemy.

- Shloka 6.26

yato yato niścalati manaś cañcalam asthiram
tatas tato niyamyaitad ātmany eva vaśaṁ nayet

From wherever the mind wanders due to its flickering and unsteady nature, one must certainly withdraw it and bring it back under the control of the Self.

- Shloka 6.35

śrī-bhagavān uvāca
asaṁśayaṁ mahā-bāho mano durnigrahaṁ calam
abhyāsena tu kaunteya vairāgyeṇa ca gṛhyate

Lord Sri Krishna said: O mighty-armed son of Kunti, it is undoubtedly very difficult to curb the restless mind, but it is possible by suitable practice and by detachment.

NOTES

1. Alana Semuels, 'We Are All Accumulating Mountains of Things', The Atlantic, https://www.theatlantic.com/technology/archive/2018/08/online-shopping-and-accumulation-of-junk/567985/.
2. Joseph P. Allen, 'Summary of Scientific Results', *Apollo 15 Prelimiary Science Report,* NASA SP, p. 2-11.
3. 'Newton's Philosophiae Naturalis Principia Mathematica', Stanford Encyclopedia of Philosophy, 20 December 2007, https://plato.stanford.edu/entries/newton-principia/
4. 'June 1798: Cavendish weighs the world', APS News, June 2008, https://www.aps.org/publications/apsnews/200806/upload/June-2008-Volume-17-Number-6-Entire-Issue.pdf.
5. Jeremy Deaton, 'Einstein Showed Newton Was Wrong About Gravity. Now Scientists Are Coming for Einstein', MACH, 3 August 2019, https://www.nbcnews.com/mach/science/einstein-showed-newton-was-wrong-about-gravity-now-scientists-are-ncna1038671.
6. Ethan Siegel, 'No, We Haven't Solved The Drake Equation, The Fermi Paradox, Or Whether Humans Are Alone', Forbes, https://www.forbes.com/sites/startswithabang/2018/06/26/no-we-cannot-know-whether-humans-are-alone-in-the-universe/?sh=6d90cc487d3b.
7. Sadhu Brahmaviharidas, 'Limitations of Perception', BAPS Swaminarayan Sanstha, https://www.baps.org/Article/2011/Limitations-Of-Perception-2150.aspx.
8. Daniel Culpan, 'Microwave Oven Baffled Astronomers for Decades', Wired, 5 may 2015, https://www.wired.co.uk/article/microwave-parkes-observatory.

9. Jessie Szalay, 'Piltdown Man: Infamous Fake Fossil', Livescience, 30 September 2016, https://www.livescience.com/56327-piltdown-man-hoax.html.
10. Corinne Reichert, 'Jeff Bezos Reclaims World's Richest Title from Elon Musk', cnet, 16 Febraury 2021, https://www.cnet.com/news/jeff-bezos-reclaims-worlds-richest-title-from-elon-musk/.
11. Siobhan Kelleher Kukolic, 'Between Stimulus and Response There Is A Space', Thrive Global, https://thriveglobal.com/stories/between-stimulus-and-response-there-is-a-space/.
12. Jill Suttie, 'Kids Do Better on the Marshmallow Test When They Cooperate', Greater Good Magazine, 24 February 2020, https://greatergood.berkeley.edu/article/item/kids_do_better_on_the_marshmallow_test_when_they_cooperate.
13. 'COVID-19 responsible for at least 3 million excess deaths in 2020', World Health Organization, 20 May 2021, https://www.who.int/news-room/spotlight/the-impact-of-covid-19-on-global-health-goals.
14. 'COVID Crisis Sinks Global Economy in 2020, Collapsing GDP 4.9%: IMF', Bangkok Post, 24 June 2020, https://www.bangkokpost.com/world/1940428/covid-crisis-sinks-global-economy-in-2020-collapsing-gdp-4-9-imf.
15. Tim Folger, 'Will Indonesia Be Ready for the Next Tsunami?', National Geographic, 28 September 2018, https://www.nationalgeographic.com/science/article/141226-tsunami-indonesia-catastrophe-banda-aceh-warning-science.
16. Jeyhun Aliyev, 'Chernobyl disaster liquidators recall horrors of nuclear accident', Anadolu Agency, 26 April 2021, https://www.aa.com.tr/en/europe/chernobyl-disaster-liquidators-recall-horrors-of-nuclear-accident/2221276.
17. 'Conducting Miller-Urey Experiments', *Journal of Visualized Experiments,* 21 January 2014, https://www.ncbi.nlm.nih.gov/pmc/articles/PMC4089479/.
18. Jayadvaita Swami, 'How Much Are You worth?', Jayadvaita Swami personal site, 22 January 2006, https://www.jswami.info/worth/.
19. Jeff Sanny, Samuel J Ling and William Moebs, 'De Broglie's

Matter Waves', *University Physics Volume 3,* Open Stax, https://opentextbc.ca/universityphysicsv3openstax/chapter/de-broglies-matter-waves/.

20. Catherine Elsworth, 'Woman Comes Back to Life After Being Dead for 17 Hours', The Telegraph, 26 May 2008, https://www.telegraph.co.uk/news/newstopics/howaboutthat/2032591/Woman-comes-back-to-life-after-being-dead-for-17-hours.html.
21. Manny Fernandez, 'Texas Woman Is Taken Off Life Support After Order', The New York Times, 26 January 2014, https://www.nytimes.com/2014/01/27/us/texas-hospital-to-end-life-support-for-pregnant-brain-dead-woman.html.
22. Mike Celizic, 'Pronounced Dead, Man Takes "Miraculous" Turn', TODAY, 24 March 2008, https://www.today.com/news/pronounced-dead-man-takes-miraculous-turn-2D80555113.
23. P van Lommel, R van Wees, V Meyers, I Elfferich, 'Near-Death Experience in Survivors of Cardiac Arrest: A Prospective Study in the Netherlands', National Library of Medicine, https://pubmed.ncbi.nlm.nih.gov/11755611/.
24. Rudolf H. Smit, 'Corroboration of the Dentures Anecdote Involving Veridical Perception in a Near-Death Experience', Merkawah Foundation, IANDS, https://citeseerx.ist.psu.edu/viewdoc/download?doi=10.1.1.1074.5800&rep=rep1&type=pdf.
25. Satwant Pasricha and Ian Stevenson, 'Indian Cases of the Reincarnation Type Two Generations Apart', University of Virginia website, https://med.virginia.edu/perceptual-studies/wp-content/uploads/sites/360/2016/12/STE25.pdf.
26. Cagda Erzincan, 'Many Lives, Many Masters—Dr. Brian L. Weiss: Discovering Your Past Lives in Dublin in May', The Circular, 13 April 2015, https://thecircular.org/many-lives-many-masters-dr-brian-l-weiss-discovering-your-past-lives-in-dublin-in-may/.
27. John Baez, 'Surprises in Logic', UC Riverside, Department of Mathematics, 4 April 2016, https://math.ucr.edu/home/baez/surprises.html.
28. https://vedicheritage.gov.in/en/vedic-chanting-unesco/.

BIBLIOGRAPHY

1. Bhaktivedantha Vedabase, the Bhagavad Gita, https://vedabase.io/en/library/bg/.
2. Bhaktivedantha Vedabase, Shrimad Bhagavatam (Bhagavata Purana) Canto 6.6.38–39, https://vedabase.io/en/library/sb/6/6/38-39/.
3. Catherine Chalmers, Gordon Grice and Michael L. Sand, *Food Chain: Encounters Between Mates, Predators and Prey*, Aperture; 1st edition, 15 April 2000.
4. J. Harrington, 'A Century of War: A Citizen's Call to Action', *International Journal on World Peace*, 19(3), pp. 91–93.
5. Iskcon Vrindavan, Vaikuntha Rasa, https://iskconvrindavan.com/20*19/09/19/vaikuntha-rasa/.*
6. S. Krishnananda, commentary on the Mundaka Upanishad, Verse 3.1.9, https://www.swamikrishnananda.org/mundak1/mundak1_5.html.
7. S. Blackman, 'Why Health Warnings Can Be Bad', 2019, https://www.ft.com/content/0d9499ec-2d75-11de-9eba-00144feabdc0.
8. Mundaka Upanishad Verse 3.1.9, https://vaniquotes.org/wiki/Mundaka_Upanisad.
9. R. Singh, 'What is your duty?' 2020, https://gyanalogy.com/what-is-your-duty/.
10. S. Sitarama Sastri, *Mundaka Upanishad With Shankara's Commentary,* 1905, https://www.wisdomlib.org/hinduism/book/mundaka-upanishad-shankara-bhashya/d/doc145122.html.
11. K. Sreedharan, 'The Science of Mundaka Upanishad', *Articles on Hinduism*, 18 June 2017, https://www.indiadivine.org/science-mundaka-upanishad/.
12. Monica Tan, 'Microwave Oven to Blame for Mystery Signal That

Left Astronomers Stumped', *The Guardian,* 5 May 2015, https://www.theguardian.com/science/2015/may/05/microwave-oven-caused-mystery-signal-plaguing-radio-telescope-for-17-years.
13. Translated by Horace Hayman Wilson, Vishnu Purana, 1840, https://www.sacred-texts.com/hin/vp/vp077.htm.
14. Valmiki Ramayana, https://www.valmiki.iitk.ac.in/content?language=ro&field_kanda_tid=2&field_sarga_value=33&field_sloka_value=12.
15. P. Van Lommel, R. Van Wees, V. Meyers, I. Elfferich, 'Near-death experience in survivors of cadiac arrest: a prospective study in the Netherlands', *The Lancet,* 2001, Issue 358, Volume (9298), pp. 2039–2045, https://www.thelancet.com/journals/lancet/article/PIIS0140673601071008/fulltext.
16. S.V. Vidyalaya, 'The Significance of 108 in Hinduism', http://www.svvtt.com/significance-of-108.html.
17. Chaitanya Charan, 'What a Saint Learned From a Prostitute', 2015, https://www.thespiritualscientist.com/2015/02/what-a-saint-learned-from-a-prostitute-2/.
18. 'Our Understanding of Karma Needs to Be Overhauled', 19 July 2021, https://jneyam.com/dharma/our-understanding-of-karma-needs-to-be-overhauled/.
19. L.H. Whitesides, 'Even Astronauts Commit Suicide: A Tribute to a Friend and a Plea', *Wired,* 2007, https://www.wired.com/2007/09/suicide-and-hom/.
20. N. Wolchover, 'How Gödel's Proof Works', *Quantamagazine,* 14 July 2020, https://www.quantamagazine.org/how-godels-incompleteness-theorems-work-20200714/.